AS I RECALL

AS I RECALL

A Bevin Boy's Story

DEREK HOLLOWS

BREWIN BOOKS

First published by
Brewin Books Ltd, 56 Alcester Road,
Studley, Warwickshire B80 7LG in 2008
www.brewinbooks.com

ISBN: 978-1-85858-415-7

A Cataloguing in Publication Record
for this title is available from the British Library

Typeset in Bembo
Printed in Great Britain by
The Alden Press.

CONTENTS

DEDICATION

This book is dedicated to my dear wife, Maureen, who encouraged me to record some of my experiences as a Bevin Boy in the Lancashire coalfield, to my supportive family and to all miners and members of our 'Forgotten Army'.

As I struggled for countless hours trying to master the art of the electric typewriter, I was blessed by the presence of our much-loved Shih Tzu, Mysha, who patiently sat at my side. She is sorely missed but now with us in spirit. To her, I owe so much.

The work is also dedicated to future generations who, at the mention of our name, may justifiably remark, "Bevin Boys? Never heard of them."

I trust that in some small way, my contribution will help enlighten them.

ACKNOWLEDGEMENTS

Joyce and Ruth Batchelor, 'Bevin Boys 1', 'Bevin Boys 2' and Standard

Mrs. Broom and Mrs. R. Rowan, Photographs and directives (Francis Broom)

John Etty, D.M.A., A.I.S.W., Foreword

Ian Winstanley, Jeff Simm, Photographs and information from their book
   'Mining Memories'

National Mining Museum Wakefield, Photographs and N.C.B. Flag

Wayne Ankers, Manchester Evening News, Photographs (John Etty)

Wakefield Express, Photographs (John Etty)

Mike Wilson, Derby City. F.C. Historian, Information (Brian Clough)

Mr. Bache, Photograph (F.O. Donald Smith)

Bill Bennett, Drawing (Snap-time)

R. Fishwick, 'Playing it safe'

Michael Alty, B.A. Hons. Photographs (Author and Medals) and script appraisal

Alexandra Wootton, Script appraisal

Mrs. Sylvia Wood, Designer, Bevin Boys Association Banner

ABOUT THE AUTHOR

Derek Hollows was born in Warrington and attended Oakwood Avenue Primary School, the Boteler Grammar School, Pinner's Brow and later, the Boteler Grammar School, Latchford.

In 1944, he was conscripted into the mines as a Bevin Boy and served at Lyme Colliery, Haydock. He completed his service as a coalface worker.

Upon his release, he qualified as a secondary school teacher and taught in both Primary and Secondary schools in the Warrington area. After gaining further teaching experience in various parts of the country, he settled in the Trafford area and retired as a head teacher.

FOREWORD

In 1945, I was accepted for service in the Royal Navy but as with so many others, I was conscripted into the mines.

I trained at the Prince of Wales Colliery, Pontefract, where I attended lectures in mining procedures and safety and participated in strenuous physical education. Underground instruction taught me about general haulage-work, how to lay and repair rail-tracks and how to care for the pit-ponies.

Upon completion of my training, the late Eddie Waring. well-known Rugby League correspondent and future T.V. commentator, arranged for me to begin my mining employment at Shawcross Colliery, Dewsbury.

On one occasion, I accidentally knocked over my oil-lamp and was enveloped in total darkness. I dare not move for my escape route was blocked by a moving conveyor-belt laden with coal. Finally, an official came to my aid but he made a point of checking my lamp to determine if the casing was cold and it was. Had it been warm, he might well have assumed that I was malingering and had deliberately extinguished it just before his arrival on the scene.

Later, I transferred to the Caphouse Colliery, Wakefield, where the National Mining Museum for England now stands and I served there until my release in 1948.

Left: John in Oldham's Hall of Fame. Right: John at the Wembley Stadium playing before 60,000 spectators. Result: Wakefield Trinity 38pts, Hull 5 pts.

I have great respect for the miners. They worked very hard, often in very bad conditions. Toilets and washing-facilities were non-existent. To say the least, it was primitive. Above all, I admired them for their resilience and courage.

John Etty, D.M.A., A.I.S.W.

John was educated at Batley Grammar School which produced such notables as Joseph Priestley, the eminent scientist who discovered oxygen and Frank Sykes, the British Lions winger.

At an early age, he was the mascot for his father's amateur Rugby League team. Later, John turned professional and played for Dewsbury, Batley, Oldham and Wakefield Trinity. As a young player, he was reserve for the England team and represented Yorkshire County and the British Empire.

In 1960, he was presented with the Rugby League Challenge Cup Winners' Medal by Her Majesty, Queen Elizabeth II, to complete his collection of winners' medals in all seven major competitions, During his sporting career, he played opposite some of the game's legends – Brian Bevan, Alex Murphy, Billy Boston and Van Hollenhoven and alongside Neil Fox, Alan Davies and Derek Turner.

For a period of forty-one years, John was engaged in social work and was appointed to senior posts in various parts of the country. He was the Deputy Director (Welfare), Middlesbrough where he was Chairman of Sports for the Disabled Association and served on the Race Relations Committee. He then became the Deputy Director (Social Services) in Blackpool. Prior to his retirement, he was the Chief Administrative Officer (Social Services), Lancashire County Council.

Over the years, John and his wife, Kath, have been involved in voluntary work for the disabled and elderly, caring for groups of them on holiday in Germany, the U.S.A. and England. Both continue to maintain an active interest in supporting the Social Services Retired Group locally.

1. INNOCENCE

As seven and eight year old children, my friends and I enjoyed visiting the local barracks, home to the South Lancashire Regiment, (The Prince of Wales' Volunteers). The main attraction was the sports field and a group of us regularly attended football matches between teams of soldiers. During one particular game, a player was stretchered off after receiving a leg injury. From that day, we all arrived in our football boots in the forlorn hope that one of us might be called upon to substitute some unfortunate. After all, we reasoned, we were their most loyal supporters. Hope springs eternal in a child's breast and there was always another day and another match to be played. Our aspirations never materialised. Looking back, the likelihood of our presenting a threat to eleven strong, fighting-fit men was minimal unless, of course, we had run between and under their legs.

Some years later, the Barracks was the scene of a more poignant display. In late May, 1940, that same group of young teenagers stood opposite the main gate. The successful rescue of our Forces from the Dunkirk beaches had been effected. We noted the arrival of three coaches. A young officer with his arm in a sling, stepped down from the leading vehicle. Slowly the transports emptied as a number of soldiers emerged. Most of them were walking-wounded. Their uniforms were dishevelled, their heads hung low and their shoulders drooped. Their gaunt faces spoke volumes and they presented a picture of extreme weariness and utter dejection. It was a pitiful sight to behold. I noticed that many of the adults around us were wiping away tears of sorrow. Suddenly, from the third coach, there came the skirl of bagpipes and out stepped a Cameron piper. His khaki tunic and kilt were heavily mud-stained and his head was swathed in a blood-stained bandage. As he marched up and down in front of the lines of men, we witnessed a remarkable change in them. They raised their heads, straightened their backs and marched smartly through the barrack gate. Later we learned that the wounded were taken to a local military hospital.

The experience made a deep impression on my friends and myself. Now we were teenagers and there was a distinct possibility that in the not-too-distant future, we would be called upon to make our contribution.

With this in mind, I turned to my friend, Eric.

"What do you want to be?" I asked.

"A soldier like him" and pointing at the departing piper, he added.

"And I want to join the Cameron Highlanders."

Four years later, his wish was realised and he became a Cameron with the 51st Highland Division. At the time, I hadn't any idea which was my preferred Service but on a Saturday afternoon in September, 1940 and aged fourteen years, I felt that the decision was made for me.

I decided to visit my grandparents who lived some five miles away. It was ideal weather for cycling and as I passed through the town centre, I could hear the cheers of the spectators who were watching a rugby league match at the Wilderspool Stadium, Warrington. With half of my journey completed, I stopped for a rest. I propped my bicycle against a wall, took a drink from my flask and looked across the River Mersey at the Thames Board Mills Factory. A fete had been organised in an adjoining field and the happy laughter of children echoed across the murky waters. In such uncertain times, it was gratifying to know that there remained some semblance of normality. I then became aware of the sound of an approaching aircraft. Gazing skyward, I saw an old, fabric-clad aeroplane which bore friendly French roundels on the wings and fuselage. "Just another war machine snatched from the Germans", I thought. It swooped so low over my head that I could clearly see the pilot at the controls. It headed for the factory. Obviously, this was a gesture by the Forces to make the fete more interesting, I felt. The excitement of the children was loud and clear. I could hear their joyful shouts and the clapping of hands as they anticipated the added treat of an air-display.

Then came the moment of horror which I can never forget. Once over the field, the airman discharged three black objects, which whistled down and exploded among these innocents. For several minutes, there was an unearthly silence, followed by cries of pain and calls for assistance. Sixteen people, including children, were killed and more than fifty were seriously wounded. On a personal note, a family friend who was in attendance, was permanently blinded. A nearby Sunday school became a temporary mortuary, During the following weeks, a sombre mood prevailed among the townsfolk. I felt grief and anger at what I had seen. My decision was made. I would join the Royal Air Force.

Unlike my friend, Eric, and for various reasons, my most fervent wish did not come to fruition. I found myself conscripted as a Bevin Boy, just one of the many who had volunteered for service in the Armed Forces. We felt cheated and I suspect that Sir Winston Churchill, himself a military man, appreciated our feelings and afforded us some consolation when he magnanimously declared, "When your grandchildren ask you what did you do to win this inheritance for us and to make our names so respected among men, you in your turn will say with equal pride and with equal right, 'We got the coal'."

SUFFER LITTLE CHILDREN

A lazy sun, a joyous day
And the silvery laughter of children at play.
War is distant, so it seems
But very soon lie shattered dreams.

Whistling shapes wing down from above.
Not doves with leaves of peace and love.
The air is stilled, no longer cheers.
What follows then stirs all our fears.

Screams arise above the din,
Innocence destroyed, a mortal sin.
A dreadful sight will take its toll
For burning anger darkens my soul.

A lazy sun, a joyous day
And the silvery laughter of children at play.
Then gone as they pass through Heaven's door
But remembered each one, forevermore.

D. Hollows

2. THE BALLOT

At the outbreak of World War Two, many young miners of military age left the mines to join the various Services. There was an urgent need for coal coupled with a depleted work-force. In 1943, Mr. Ernest Bevin, Minister of Labour in the Coalition Government. stated at a miners' conference in Blackpool that a shortage of coal could prolong the war.

The situation was so serious that he introduced a system of ballot. The numbers 0 to 9 were recorded on slips of paper which were placed in a hat. A secretary made the draw. If the number or numbers selected coincided with the last digit or digits of one's National Service number, one could expect to be directed to the industry. This method of selection was ongoing at regular intervals from December, 1943 until April, 1945.

A wide cross-section of society was recruited by this innovation. Among them, were tradesmen, shop-assistants, accountants, officer-cadets and students. Some were destined to become household names – Eric Morecambe, Sir James Savile and Nat Lofthouse, Bolton and England centre-forward, known as the Lion of Vienna, to name but a few.

There was much resentment among ballotees who had been pronounced medically-fit and wished to join the Armed Forces. Indeed, many had served as Cadets in preparation for acceptance into a branch of the Services. Tribunals were set up where objections could be voiced but a firm directive had been issued which would not be rescinded. It was a fait-accompli and the die had been cast.

3. TRAINING AND DIRECTIVES

Wherever possible, the Bevin Boys were sent to training centres within close proximity of collieries. There, they were kitted out with safety-helmets, safety-boots and overalls.

For a period of four weeks, they were introduced to surface and underground systems, received instruction in mine-safety and participated in physical education to develop muscle tone.

They were then directed to various coal mines throughout the country and after a few weeks of surface training, they went underground.

MINISTRY OF LABOUR AND NATIONAL SERVICE

Emergency Powers (Defence) Acts, 1939-1941

DIRECTION ISSUED UNDER REGULATION 58A OF THE DEFENCE (GENERAL) REGULATIONS, 1939.

NOTE.—Any person failing to comply with a direction under Regulation 58A of the Defence (General) Regulations, 1939, is liable on summary conviction to imprisonment for a term not exceeding three months, or to a fine not exceeding £100 or to both such imprisonment and such fine. Any person failing to comply after such a conviction is liable on a further conviction to a fine not exceeding five pounds for every day on which the failure continues.

To F.Broom

58, Meville St.,

Liverpool 8.

MINISTRY OF LABOUR
GOVT. TRAINING CENTRE
(Date) 18 APR 1944
CRAMLINGTON

In pursuance of Regulation 58A of the Defence (General) Regulations, 1939, I, the undersigned, a National Service Officer within the meaning of the said Regulations, do hereby direct you to perform the services specified by the Schedule hereto (see overleaf) being services which, in my opinion, you are capable of performing.

If you become subject to the provisions of an Essential Work Order in the employment specified in the Schedule, the direction will cease to have effect and your right to leave the employment will be determined under that Order. Otherwise, this direction continues in force until 17 OCT 1944 or until withdrawn by a National Service Officer.

I hereby withdraw all directions previously issued to you under Regulation 58A of the said Regulations and still in force.

National Service Officer.

E.D. 883A.

[P.T.O.

SCHEDULE

Employment %K in or about a coal mine

with   The Ashington Coal Co.Ltd.
at   Ellington Colliery.

under instruction and supervision provided for in
Article 2 (l)(a)(i) of the Coal Mining (Training &
%% Medical Examination) Order 1944 with a view to
employment on work below ground.
beginning on___24th April 1944___19__

particulars of which are as follows :—
The rate of remuneration and conditions of service will be

agreed district rate and conditions.

Further particulars Travel on 24th April 1944 from the
Haymarket Bus Station at 9.0 a.m arriving Ashington
at 10.0 a.m when you should report to the Employment
Exchange Ashington.

Left: Specific Colliery Directive. Right: Destination – Ellington.

ACCOMMODATION

Hostel and private accommodation were provided for Bevin Boys who were unable
to travel home every day. Railways warrants were also issued.

NATIONAL SERVICE ACTS

GRADE CARD.

Registration No. LLB52969

Mr. Francis Broom

whose address on his registration card is
39 Grenville St.
Liverpool 8

was medically examined on 31.12.43

at   LIVERPOOL
            MEDICAL   5

and placed in

GRADE*   I One

Chairman of Board   wonalin

Medical Board stamp

Man's Signature   F Broom

*The roman numeral denoting the man's Grade (with number
also spelt out) will be entered in RED ink by the Chairman himself,
e.g., Grade I (one) Grade II (two) (a) (Vision).

N.S. 55.   [P.T.O.

NATIONAL SERVICE HOSTELS CORPORATION LIMITED

ASHINGTON   MINERS   HOSTEL

MEMBERSHIP CARD

NAME FRANCIS   BROOM
NATIONAL REGISTRATION No. M.H.L.A 96 3.
ROOM No. B. 40   KEY. 803
CARD No. 577
DATE OF ISSUE 18.5.46

Left: Medical Card. Top Right: Bevin Boy, Francis Broom.
Bottom Right: Ashington Miner's Hostel.

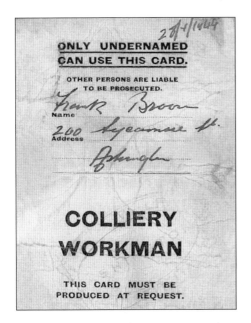
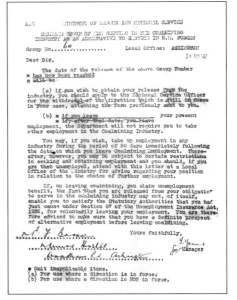

Top Left: Band of brothers. Top Right: Sea air clears the lungs. Centre Left: Better up here than down there. Centre Right: Bevin Boy musician. Bottom Left: Ashington Miners' Welfare Institute (Member's Card). Bottom Right: Release from National Service.

4. WHAT, NO UNIFORM?

During the conflict, all United Kingdom citizens were issued with a National Registration Identity Card which, in the case of those employed in the mining industry, was endorsed by the Ministry of Labour and National Service.

It is not generally known that being a Bevin Boy had its disadvantages. They did not wear the King's uniform. Some considered them to be conscientious objectors and there were instances of certain members receiving white feathers. Others were arrested on suspicion of being deserters or enemy agents and were questioned by the authorities.

Many had to endure comments about not doing their duty for King and country. To impressionable teenagers, such criticism could be both embarrassing and hurtful. Little did their accusers know of the daily demands and dangers faced by these boys when they descended into the bowels of the earth.

Until nationalisation in 1947, Lyme Colliery, Haydock, Lancashire, was owned by the Richard Evans Company which had interests in coal mines all over the area.

Lyme Colliery, Haydock in 1936. (Pictures courtesy of Mr. Simm).

5. THE DREADED DROP

The lowering and raising of the cage was controlled by a skilled operator in the winding-house. In some mines, cages had plummeted to the pit-bottom, killing the occupants. Fortunately, such incidents were rare.

One of the most traumatic experiences for the newly-arrived Bevin Boy was that first descent into the abyss.

For the first few yards, the movement of the cage was slow but apprehension became all too evident when speeds of over sixty miles per hour were reached. Reactions varied. The pressure could cause a blocking of the ears which could be relieved by swallowing. Some poor unfortunates suffered from nose-bleeds and others felt physically sick.

A young Bevin Boy summed up the feelings of so many when he declared, "The cage dropped so fast that this morning's breakfast met last night's supper."

The miners were well-aware of the anxieties experienced by their new protégés and tried to dissipate their fears through humour.

On one occasion, as the cage plunged down the shaft, a collier shouted above the noise, "Reet, lads, t'first floor's clothin' an' t'second floor's soft-furnishin's." He looked at a trembling, pale-faced Bevin Boy and added, "Not to worry, son. Toilets are on t'next floor."

ADVICE TO NEW RECRUITS

Thy numbers 'ave come up, lads, make no mistake abaht that.
Cheer up, tha'll look reet dapper, lads, wi' thy lamp, boots an' new 'at.
We got t'get more coal out to save our pleasant land,
So now tha can tell th'ole world tha's one o' Bevin's Band.
There's nowt tha can do abaht it, so take it on thy chin,
Everyone's gorra job to do if this war we're goin' t'win.

T'sensation that'll get in t'cage, lads, is reet out o'this world.
Las' week, a chap brought up 'is grub as downward 'e were 'urled.
Another one 'ad poppin' ears but ' swallered an' it went,
Then 'is mate, poor lad, did summat worse an' left an awful scent.
For a few 'air-raisin' moments, 'e thowt t'cage 'd never stop,
Cos 'e felt 'is feet at t'bottom an' t'rest of 'im on top.

Arrived at last, step out, lads an' then 'and in thy tally:
It's light down theer, a busy place, so do not dilly-dally.
Gerra good whiff o' that bracin' air, pre-'istory at its best.
Forget the 'ard work facin' thee. At snap, tha gets a rest.
That's when we all sit down an' crack a joke or two,
Keeps us goin', tha knows, for pleasures 'ere are few.

Tunnels may be low, lads, so it's wise t'duck thy 'ead.
An' if tha's tall, make thysen small an' curl up like tha does in bed.
Don't tha worry abaht roof-falls. They 'appen every day.
Remember tha's doin' owd Bevin proud, as 'e 'issen would say
An' when tha's served thy time, my boys, then an' only then,
Tha can proudly say, "We went down as lads an' come back up as men."

D. Hollows

6. A SMALL TRIBUTE

In 1944 and straight from the Boteler Grammar School, Warrington, I received my initial training at the Newtown Colliery, Swinton, Manchester and was then directed to Gresford Colliery, Wrexham. Within a matter of days, the order was countermanded and I was sent to the Lyme Pit, Haydock, Lancs, where I served until 1947.

Having volunteered for aircrew duties at the age of sixteen and having been rejected because of my age, my initial reaction to working underground was full of misgivings. However, I soon learned to respect this rare breed of men who daily toiled in dark and dangerous conditions. They became my friends, encouraging me at all times and giving me their full support. It was a privilege to become an accepted member of that fraternity. In the interests of posterity, I feel it incumbent upon me to mention some of my mentors and to speak of one man in particular.

I recall so many names – Barney Woodacre, Steve Gleave, Paddy Redmond, Jimmy Wright, Tom Rigby, Arnold Goodman, George Manchester, who had a fine singing voice, Tommy Higham, who sustained severe pelvic injuries in a massive roof-fall and, finally, Spurge Green, our Deputy. He was a Haydock man, known as a "Yicker."

Spurgeon Luther Montague Green was an unforgettable character. He had given evidence at the inquiry into the 26th February, 1930, explosion when over one thousand family members and friends gathered at the pit-head, awaiting news of their loved ones. Thirteen men were killed, others were injured and badly burned. Spurge was complimented by the Panel on his initiative in maintaining underground to surface communications, thus expediting the rescue operations.

He was a small, squat, muscular man and had very bandy legs, due to their having been broken several times during rescues in various underground districts. His vocabulary, often interspersed with oaths, turned the air blue. With little thought for himself, he had saved the lives of others. To our group of Bevin Boys, he was a hero, a man to be respected and admired.

When I injured my hand, Spurge opened his First Aid tin, took out a small phial of iodine, punctured it on a rock and emptied the contents into the wound. In the dim light, he did not realise that he had ripped the gauze at the end of the phial and that he had filled the cut with small slivers of glass.

"Cheer up, lad. Tha'll soon be all reet," he assured me and slid off. Needless to say, I was 'all reet', after a few long and painful weeks.

In comparison to the many traumas suffered by Spurge, this, I felt, was nothing.

REMEMBRANCE

Not a Wordsworth, a Shelley, a Byron or Keats
But a simple tribute to long-past feats,
To the men who performed them, my memories so clear.
This humble dedication is deeply sincere.

Barney and Steve, the paternal pair,
Full of courage, compassion and selfless care:
Men without equal, men brimming with grace.
Each name shines forth in its own honoured place.

Jimmy, the fireman, who trained us all
And Tommy, the driller, sore-maimed in a fall.
Spurge Green, a true hero in Yicker eyes,
Shoring restless Earth to save men's lives.

Big George, the one with the gifted voice:
To hear him sing made one's soul rejoice.
Mac, the shot-firer, Paddy, old Tom,
Dripping sweat, rippling muscles, now sadly all gone.

Yet yesteryear, they lived, laughed and breathed
And to those who knew them, their strengths they bequeathed
I think of them just as they were then.
So thank you, dear friends. May God bless you. Amen.

Yicker: a native of Haydock, Lancashire.

D. Hollows

7. COURAGE AND COMPASSION

Many of the miners with whom I worked had witnessed the dreadful injuries suffered by the victims after the explosion in 1930 at the Lyme Colliery, Haydock.

They paid tribute to Dr. Dowling, to Miss Bone, Matron of the Haydock Cottage Hospital and especially so to the young Dr. Winifred Bridges, a local practitioner. The tragedy initiated her first venture underground. Accompanied by Dr. Dowling, she set to with a will and helped tend the injured. She became a local heroine and was held in high regard by all who were fortunate enough to know her.

In the 1940's and on a daily basis, nature did not allow us to forget that terrible mishap. As we descended, we passed the entrance to the old workings where the explosion had occurred. We were forever aware of the smell of burnt timber which lingered in the air and exuded into the main shaft. For my colleagues and myself, it served as a constant reminder of the dangers that forever lurked beneath the surface.

The years passed without a major incident but in 1949, just as the night-shift was going off duty, there was another explosion which blew out a massive stopping.

Five men from the Boothstown Rescue Team went underground but sadly, two of them lost their lives. For their bravery that night, a British Empire Medal and several George Medals were awarded by King George the Sixth to those who had participated.

8. A LAMENT

I was so proud of those safety-boots. To a callow youth, accustomed only to shoes, plimsolls and football boots, they represented an innovation masterminded by craftsmen. Pitted leather uppers, sturdy soles and above all, shining steel toe-caps heralded my arrival in a new and exciting working world.

"They're reet good boots, them," commented Barney, my underground mentor and work-mate. "Should last thee a lifetime," he added and my chest swelled with pride at the compliment. "Be sure to grease 'em on t'machine when tha's finished t'shift. Preserves 'em, y'know," he continued and I followed his advice religiously.

Those boots meant so much to me. No more pieces of shaped cardboard fitted inside worn leather soles, a ritual frequently performed during austere times. Such running repairs were fine in dry weather and on flat surfaces, of course.

Six weeks after going underground, I was travelling to work for the afternoon shift. It was a bitterly cold day as I entered the railway compartment which was very warm and welcoming. For security, I would normally place the boots round my neck but on that freezing afternoon, I breached my habitual rule by gently placing them on the rack above my head, I was the sole occupant but on reflection, would have appreciated some companionship to keep me alert. The train drew out of Bank Quay Station, Warrington and with the relaxing heat around me and the rhythm of the wheels beneath, I fell into a deep sleep.

I awoke with a start to hear a voice shout, "Now leaving Earlestown. Close your doors please." Earlestown was my destination. Without a thought, I jumped up, opened the door and shot out on to the platform just as the train pulled off down the track. "Ee, lad, you cut it fine then," observed a porter. Somehow, I felt incomplete, half-dressed, in fact, and it registered that my prized boots were slipping away. Unable to retrieve them, I advised the porter of my loss. "Don't think you'll be seeing them again, son. Everyone needs good footwear nowadays. Still, I'll phone down the line but you'll be lucky to get 'em back." So it was. They were gone forever.

I changed into my underground clothes in the locker-room.

"Weer's tha boots, laddie?" Barney asked.

"I've left them on the train," I moaned.

"Well, what's tha goin' down wi'?"

"My shoes. I've nothing else," I answered.

"Not so wise to wear 'em but I reckon they'll 'ave to do," said Barney and added, "Tell you what... If tha comes early t'morrow, I'll take thee t'cloggers. You can't beat clogs. T'chap will measure tha feet and make 'em to perfection. Oh, aye, tha'll need clips on t'top. Easy to get'em off if tha foot gets trapped." With Barney's help which was much appreciated, the transaction was finally completed. Now all I had to do was wait.

But what of that interim period between losing my boots and picking up my clogs? My only pair of shoes had been virtually ruined and I now had to find alternative footwear fast. Salvation came in the shape of a pair of football boots from my schooldays. They were more accustomed to grass and mud than to rock and coal but they would serve their purpose. "Take out the studs for comfort and those toe-caps are solid. Better than nothing," I mused.

The following day, I presented myself for work wearing my modified soccer-boots.

"Not much better than them shoes," quipped Barney. "Might 'ave a pit team after t'war an' tha'll all be geared up to play. That's if tha keeps thee eyes open an' don't damage thysen in a fall." In response, I smiled and shivered a little as I still do when I recall my being trapped on the coalface several years later but that is another story. I certainly received plenty of attention from the other lads with their diverse, good-humoured comments such as, "Hey, Dek, kick that tub from here to yon" and "You'll pay t'penalty for wearin' them." At least, they and I knew that I had created a record. I was the first and I would think, the last to introduce a new style of underground footwear. The idea never caught on.

It was with great relief that I collected my clogs some days later. At first, they were hard on the feet but after being broken in, they were warm, substantial and extremely comfortable.

I loved the sound that they made when steel tips met hard ground. Joining my many mining friends as we clattered through the streets to the pit-head, I felt a surge of pride and very honoured to play my part in that noisy orchestra.

Many years have passed and during nostalgic moments, I reflect on the fate of those safetyboots. Surely, after all this time and assuming that they exist, they still can't adorn someone else's size ten feet. I hope that they were well cared for by their new recipient. I prefer to think of them living out their days in peaceful retirement, possibly standing as proud planters on a nature lover's garden patio and giving as much pleasure to others as they did to me so long ago.

BEVIN'S BOOTS

My heart lies heavy and full of woes,
For I loved Bevin's boots with their shiny toes.
Alas, they have gone down the rail-road track
And I feel quite certain they won't be back.

You can't go under with two bare feet,
So I've been to the clog-shop just down the street.
I still miss those boots, now a thing of the past
But proud I stand, a true miner at last.

D. Hollows

9. JUDGE NOT

During my early days as a Bevin Boy, I travelled from home and frequented a local newsagent's to purchase a newspaper. The vendor was an elderly, friendly soul but whenever I entered, I noticed that there was a fellow who seemed to have reserved a permanent place in a corner of the shop. He had a raucous voice and chatted away to all and sundry. I felt that the shopkeeper was intimidated by him. Certainly, he was no asset to the business. I never knew his name and did not care to find out. Every statement that he made was accompanied by a loud guffaw and I noted that customers beat a hasty retreat when he was around. I felt that he would have been better employed on the forecourt as a collection-box with a hand extended, inviting contributions.

One afternoon, after a stint underground, I called in at the shop which was quite busy. Sure enough, he was there in his customary place. Suddenly, I became aware that he had fixed his eyes on me. He approached menacingly and bellowed, "Hey you, you look old enough. Why aren't you in uniform doing your bit?" Customers turned and stared. No eighteen year old enjoys being embarrassed and especially so, in front of witnesses. He went on, "What are you then, C3 or a conchie?"

"Neither," I mumbled, hanging down my head. Then, I ran from the shop.

When I reported for duty the next morning, I mentioned the incident to some of my workmates who were Bevin Boys.

"Don't let it get you down, lad." Jim said. "We get it all the time. Only last week, I floored a bloke who started on me in the street."

"Yes, but you're a big chap. You can take care of yourself," I replied, "It's a wonder I've not been floored myself before now."

"Pity they haven't given us a uniform or a badge or something," exclaimed Harry. "Maybe we're not in the front-line but there are plenty in the Forces who aren't either. Of course, they've got uniforms, so no one says anything. Blimey, that's an idea, maybe some of 'em think we're special agents, doing undercover work."

"You can say that again," Jim said. "A couple of weeks ago, a bobby stopped me and asked me what I was up to."

"Why, were you going to break in somewhere?" Harry joked.

"No chance," Jim responded. "It was because I was in civvies, that's all."

The next day, I went to pick up my paper. He was there, as usual. I made my purchase and quickly left. He followed me to the doorway and shouted after me, "Where's your uniform, mate?" I ignored him and realised that Jim's 'Take no notice' policy was beginning to pay off.

Two days later, some bricks fell down the shaft. The maintenance team examined every inch of that enormous drop. It was a slow, painstaking job and we surfaced three hours later than normal. There wasn't any question of my taking a shower as I had to catch my transport home.

I popped into the news-agent's, wearing my pit-clothes, helmet and clogs. I was covered in black dust and although probably he could only see the whites of my eyes, my tormentor recognised me all right. This time, he was stuck for words, his mouth agape. Knowing that I had caught him off-balance, my confidence grew by the second.

I walked up to him, stared hard at him and said, "War's a dirty business, isn't it?"

He nodded in assent.

"Were you in the 14–18 war?" I asked.

"Too young" he replied.

"And what about this one?" I continued.

"Oh, er, bad feet and back trouble" he responded.

"I think you've got something else too" I said.

"What's that?" he asked.

"Big mouth trouble," I replied and I left the shop, my clogs clattering loudly down the street. Justice had been served and I was a very, very happy young man.

10. PIT-BROW LASSES

Fortunately, the days when women and children slaved underground have been consigned to history. However, since those times, successive generations of females in the coalfields have continued to support their male counterparts in an alternative capacity but now on the surface.

Known as "pit-brow lasses", they worked in the screening-plants where the coal was cleaned and graded. One was forever aware of the good-natured chit-chat that was part of their daily routine and of the spirit of camaraderie that existed between them.

Small wonder that the miners appreciated their contribution for the role of the lasses was of paramount importance.

A collier once pronounced, "In all t'years I've been down t'pit, I 'aven't yet seen a lass wi' a miserable face," to which his companion retorted, "That's cos they don't work down t'pit no more." "Aye," came the reply, "But if push 'appened t'come to shove an' there was no chaps t'win t'coal, they'd be down 'ere like a shot an' they'd still be smilin'."

HOMAGE

Grimy hands, sorting and scratching:
A job well done, their final goal.
Rhythmic movements, matching, snatching,
Eyes alert for rock and coal.

Hard to speak in that dusty place,
Humming and buzzing with endless noise.
Blackened and hooded, they stand with grace,
Female forms with elegant poise.

Smiling, cheerful, supporting their men,
Women at war all play their part.
Bodies tire and weary but then,
All that they do is with good heart.

Endless days and hours are long,
Heads bent low, the picking goes on.
Come faint echoes of a happy song.
Then all join in and sound as one.

From darkened faces, one sees a glow.
The sweat of toil will come and pass.
When day is done and warm waters flow,
We will see the beauty of the pit-brow lass.

D. Hollows

11. RHUBARB, RHUBARB

On the coalface, we had far too much to do to indulge in other than work-related conversation so our discussions usually took place during snap-times.

One night, Steve referred to the Dig for Victory campaign. Turning toward me, he asked "Grow anything in your garden, Dek?"

"Not much room," I replied. "The Anderson shelter takes up most of the space and that is covered in nasturtiums."

"Good for thee, an' all," advised Barney "Tha can eat t'leaves, tha knows. Taste reet good in salad."

"Grow quite a lot o' rhubarb mysen," said Steve.

"So do I," agreed Barney. "An' that's good for thee an' all. It keeps thee regular. Nowt like a bit o' stewed rhubarb."

I fully concurred with that statement. Rhubarb and custard were part and parcel of Sunday's diet. No matter how limited the garden area, the majority of folk grew a few sticks of rhubarb. I smiled to myself as I recollected an incident I had witnessed several months earlier.

Two of our neighbours were Mr. Wood and Mr. Tomkins. Both were in their seventies, The former had iron-grey hair and a matching moustache. He always wore a blue pin-striped suit and a grey homburg with a black hat-band. His cheeks were pink and his nose was extremely red. Indeed, one local teenager who had just started to learn French, irreverently called him "Nez Rouge." Mr. Wood was an inveterate pipe-smoker who nurtured his home-grown tobacco plants with great care. The obnoxious smoke that exuded from his pipe-bowl hastened the departure of any acquaintances who might meet him in the street.

Mr. Tomkins was referred to by the children as 'Grandpa Tom'. He was well over six feet tall and very thin. Invariably, he wore a brown suit with a matching flat cap. The fact that he was never without his black cycle-clips fastened to his ankles, caused some amusement for he didn't have a bicycle. It was rumoured that he went to bed in them and even wore them when he had a bath.

Mr. Wood and he were as different as chalk from cheese but they had one thing in common. They both grew rhubarb. Mr. Wood, with the larger garden, could boast a plentiful supply. In comparison, Grandpa Tom had a very small back-yard. However, he had developed a tiny plot in the far corner, which was partially bordered by a retaining wall of Victorian setts. In the midst stood his prized specimens. As youngsters, we were often invited into his yard. After negotiating the dung-heap that he built up between the rear wall and' the outdoor toilet, we would gaze in feigned awe at his well-tended rhubarb and eagerly anticipate the appearance from the kitchen of Grandma Tom who handed round the acid drops.

Promptly, at 9.20 a.m. on Mondays to Fridays and at 9.45 a.m. on Saturdays, the two men could be seen peering through their front-windows. With pocket-watches in hand, their concentration was intense. They reminded one of starters at an athletics meeting.

Then came the object of their interest in the shape of the Co-op bread-van, drawn by Henry the horse. Punctually, Arthur the bread man, would halt directly opposite the houses of the two protagonists. Day after day and in the same spot, Henry couldn't contain himself. Messrs. Wood and Tomkins with their implements, would' hasten out of their front-doors and within seconds, the manure would be transferred to their respective buckets. This would be followed by the ceremony of scattering it round the base of the plants and watering it in.

For some time, there had been angry mutterings between the pair as they collected Henry's offerings. It was apparent that this state of affairs could not continue for much longer and one morning as they performed their ritual, the bubble burst. Tempers were so frayed that they dropped their equipment on the cobble-stones and came to blows. Passers-by stared in amazement as Grandpa Tom's false teeth flew from his mouth and his spectacles were torn from his face. He was so shortsighted that he began to grapple with one of the onlookers by mistake. Mr. Wood's hat was dislodged and trampled on and his pipe and time-piece lay shattered in the gutter.

At that point, Mr. Owen, a near neighbour intervened. He stood between the opponents and commanded, "Cut it out, gentlemen. No need for this at your age. Why don't you take it in turns?"

"What do you mean, take it in turns?" Grandpa Tom wheezed.

"Well," came the response. "You collect it on Mondays, Wednesdays and Fridays and Mr. Wood can pick it up on Tuesdays, Thursdays and Saturdays." He drew the two men together, put his arms round their shoulders and called for a truce. Reluctantly, hands were shaken and the pact appeared to be sealed.

"Hold on a minute," Mr. Wood interrupted. "It's Saturday today and that lot's mine." Everyone looked down.

"What lot?" Mr. Owen asked. "Nothing there. It's gone." True enough, the pile had disappeared. One of the group pointed and cried, "Look at him, legging it." During the altercation, Willy Entwistle from the far end of the street, had taken advantage of the situation. We turned and saw him running homeward with a bucket in one hand and a shovel in the other. No doubt, he too, grew rhubarb.

During the following months, there was uneasy peace between the contenders, punctuated by sudden, sharp skirmishes.

Finally, Henry the horse was retired and his replacement, Dolly, brought the dispute to an end. In her womanly wisdom, she chose to perform the necessaries near to the stables, three miles away.

Everyone breathed a sigh of relief. Peace reigned once again. That is, until the bombs began to fall.

RHUBARB, RHUBARB

In those dark days, it was good to see
A bowl of rhubarb for Sunday tea.
Most folk had a little garden plot,
And those without, a retaining pot.

Inspecting and feeding with hand-forks and trowels,
A well-known fact it was good for the bowels:
Green leaves, red sticks growing and claiming the sun.
Digging for Victory for everyone.

With lashings of custard, a joyous treat,
Savoured, devoured, a meal complete.
So let us be grateful for Nature's forces
And never forget those magnificent horses.

12. NO SURRENDER

During the war, most people had some sort of shelter to protect them from aerial bombardment. There were Anderson shelters, brick-built surface, brick-built underground shelters, Tube stations, cellars, cupboards under stairs and certain hardy souls decided to let fate take its course and remained in bed, no doubt, with their heads under the blankets.

A group of our neighbours decided to build their own sizeable sub-surface shelter. It stood in the corner of a field behind our row of terraced houses. Constructed during the phony war, it remained unused for quite some time, except by rats and mice, Of course, children regarded it as an exciting meeting-place but none managed to enter its depths. Wary and watchful parents would admonish wayward youngsters and shout, "It could fall in. Keep out." Indeed, it had been built without official supervision and a big question mark hung over its safety.

After work and after tea, it was a ritual for Charlie, Tom and Norman to gather on the corner at the rear of our house. Tom, the leader and centre of attention, would lean against the wall and pontificate, watched by his two admirers. Charlie would puff at his pipe and nod in agreement, even when it was obvious that he disagreed. Tom and Norman would draw on their Woodbines. Sometimes, because of shortages, they had to resort to Pasha cigarettes, foul-smelling as they were. Occasionally, they would smoke leaves supplied by old Mr. Wood, who grew tobacco plants in his garden. They smelled even worse than the Pasha cigarettes.

Tom was a big man, broad-shouldered and very loud. People could hear him at the other end of the street

One evening, my parents decided to visit relatives. I settled down by the fireside to do my homework. The black-out blinds were in place and because the evening was mild, I left the back-door slightly ajar. I could hear every word uttered by the trio outside.

"I'm off for a pint," said Norman. "Good night, both. See you tomorrow."

"I'll be glad when this lot's over," Tom boomed. "It'll be great to have my lads back." One was in the Royal Navy and the other in the R.A.F.

"Me, too," agreed Charlie whose son was in the Royal Armoured Corps.

Then came the warning siren.

"Here they come," observed Tom and he continued to discuss mundane, everyday matters as if nothing untoward was happening.

"They'll soon be gone," I heard Charlie say. "They don't stay long round here." It was generally believed that the thick pall of smoke which perpetually hung over our town, afforded us some form of natural protection.

The heavy drone of laden aircraft drew closer. I went to the garden gate and saw Tom looking skyward. "Bastards," he shouted, "Do your damnedest, you won't beat us. Tell Adolph he's had it."

At that moment, a cluster of incendiaries fell. One went straight down a neighbour's chimney and both he and his wife came running out. He, in his pyjamas, carried a stirrup-pump and bucket and she, in a nightdress and her hair tied up with rag curlers, a long-handled shovel.

"Bugger it," I heard the husband shout. "There's no water in the bloody bucket" and he ran back into the house.

A display of small fires, which grew larger by the minute, appeared all around. Silhouetted against it all, I saw Tom, waving his clenched fist defiantly to the skies and bawling obscenities.

A mobile anti-aircraft unit sped round the corner and once positioned, began firing into the darkness. I could hear shrapnel hitting the ground. Tom stood unmoved by it all. "What a hero." I thought.

Then the first bomb dropped. The explosion was earth and ear shattering. I heard Tom shout, "Quick, Charlie, run for your life," but Charlie was long gone.

"One day," I thought, "I'll be up there helping to keep that lot at bay," little realising that when that day came, I would be underground as a Bevin Boy.

A second bomb exploded. It was the last I saw of Tom that night as he threw his massive frame head-first into the shelter.

"It's only fair," I reflected. "He organised its construction. He should be the first to test it out."

Two weeks later, empty and used but once by Tom, it collapsed.

NO SURRENDER

The sirens wail, comes the laden drone
Of cloud-covered craft. Not one alone.
Beams of light probe darkened skies.
Guns thunder and roar amid orders and cries.

Tom stands defiant, Woodbine 'twixt lips:
Street-corner counsellor, with hands on hips
And Norman and Charlie, his neighbours for years,
Both smoking and chatting, displaying no fears.

Then incendiaries trail like falling rain,
Clattering, bursting, with intentions so plain.
Countless fires spreading everywhere.
But our trio continues to stand and stare.

Tom shouts, "Adolf, you've had it, my son.
You won't budge me. The war's good as won.
Come on, you b........s, you can't scare me."
The air turns blue with his impropriety.

What follows next makes the whole ground quake.
Even Tom himself, begins to shake.
"Hell," he bellows, "That's a b....y big one.
Run for your life, Charlie." But he's already gone.

To a night of torment, we must again resign.
Tom looks at the sky. Gives a contemptuous sign.
Panic stations. Fearful folk run helter-skelter,
While Tom dives head-first into his home-made shelter.

13. IN THE STARS

"Manager wants to see thee in his office when tha's finished," my deputy instructed me.

The shift over, I proceeded to the Manager's office and tapped on the door.

"Come in," invited a gentle voice. To me, this was the inner sanctum. Seated behind his desk was my Manager, Mr. Lloyd Thompson. He had the manner of an unassuming and kindly man. This was the first time that I had met him face to face and I liked him immediately.

He shook my hand warmly and beckoned me to a chair.

"Do you know why I wish to see you?" he asked.

"Well, I think I do, sir," I replied.

He went on, "First of all, I want to congratulate you on winning the N.C.B. slogan competition. I have received notification from the powers that be and I know that its been reported in various newspapers. Let me say that you have brought credit to our colliery."

"Thank you," I replied, feeling a little embarrassed but rather proud. I reflected that until that time, my contribution to the industry had been minimal.

"Do you have any mining connections?" he queried. He had the capacity to put one at ease.

"I've heard my father speak of a distant cousin who was involved in the introduction of the endless rope-haulage system and devised automatic couplings for railway wagons," I answered.

Feeling much more relaxed, I continued, "I believe that his inspiration came at night as he lay in bed. He kept a note-book and pencil to hand so that he could record his ideas while they remained, fresh in his mind."

"Did you ever meet him?" Mr. Thompson asked.

"No, I didn't even know him," I went on, "The story goes that one Sunday morning, he went underground to test some new equipment. He was alone and failed to surface. A search-party found him dead."

"Sad, very sad," Mr. Thompson observed. "I seem to recall that incident from somewhere," He continued, "Sounds as if you have mining in your blood. What would you like to do when you are released?"

"I very much wish to teach," I affirmed.

"Long term ambition then?" he said.

"Since I was about nine years old," I began to reminisce. "I remember being asked that very same question by my minister, the Reverend Waddell. At the time, I had been inspired by a film I'd seen, based on the life of David Livingstone and I wanted to become a missionary. I recall Mr. Waddell saying in a broad Scots accent, 'If you want to do that sort of work, my boy, you'll have to build yourself up and no better way than getting a goodly bowl of porridge down you every morning."

The patient Mr. Thompson laughed. "And did you follow his advice?"

"Yes, sir," I replied. "I've eaten a bowl of porridge every day for the last eleven years." Again he laughed.

"I have a proposition for you, young man" he advised. "How would you like to go to Wigan Mining College to study for a mining engineer's degree? There'll always be a job for you when you've finished. Don't make a hasty decision. Just go home and think about it. There's no rush."

I felt very honoured that he had even considered me. I thanked him for his kindness, shook his hand and bade him farewell.

I considered his suggestion at great length. I felt drawn in two directions but I drafted a letter to the College and was about to post it when fate took a hand.

My younger sister who attended the local Primary School, rushed in. That day, she had been approached by her headmaster who asked, "Is it your brother who's won the National Coal Board competition? I've read about it in the paper."

"Yes, Sir, it is," she told him.

"What does he wish to do when he leaves the mine?" he questioned.

"I think he wants to be a teacher," she answered.

"Right then, tell him to come and see me as soon as he is released. I may be able to help."

I felt a pang of regret at my not having accepted Mr. Thompson's offer. He realised where my preference lay and graciously acknowledged my decision, wishing me every future success.

So it was. For some months, I worked under the guidance of my head until I proceeded to college and qualified.

In my time, I have met some wonderful people who have helped mould my life. Among them, I must name Mr. Lloyd Thompson, Manager, Lyme Colliery, Haydock and Dicky Latham, Headmaster.

14. SILENCE IS GOLDEN

Cecil was a strange man, a loner by nature and, I felt, by inclination. He worked on the regular night-shift. In the cage, he passed almost unnoticed. I do believe that none of us was aware of his actual function but this was war-time and people came and went. Wraith-like, he would appear from nowhere, muttering away to himself. He seemed like a permanent underground fixture, part and parcel of and completely in accord with that subterranean world of coal, fossils and mice. Indeed, we surmised that as he seemed reluctant to communicate with us, he did so with them. Anyone who tried to engage him in conversation would be met with a curt "Nay." That is all we could get out of him.

"All reet, Cecil?" someone asked, "Nay", came the response. It seemed that his vocabulary was severely restricted.

"Sounds like a ruddy 'orse," joked Alec.

Once, Ted observed "War's going well, i'n't, Cecil?" to which he replied "Nay" and wandered off.

"They owt to mak' 'im t'Minister of Propaganda," Alec exclaimed. "T'war would be o' er by now."

"Aye," agreed Ted, "But who'd 'ave won?" at which we all laughed.

Many years have passed and I can still visualize Cecil, picking his way along the haulage road, tapping his stick. A stick was an invaluable aid to the miner who often had to travel long distances, negotiating undulating, rocky roads and narrow tunnels.

One night, three of us were working on haulage. The track ran for approximately one hundred yards, at the end of which there was a sharp left turn. From that point, the road became more hazardous for it was steeply inclined, At the bend and to the right, there was an old air-road. This was Cecil's favourite haunt, When he disappeared, as he frequently did, we imagined him wandering for miles, muttering to himself, tapping away with his stick and ending up in the nether regions.

We noticed Cecil leave the air-road and proceed up the steep gradient. Some five minutes passed. Suddenly, we heard the loud rattle of runaway tubs. As they gathered momentum, the noise became deafening. All at once and preceding them, Cecil appeared. He took a gigantic leap into the air-road, followed by the tubs, which left the track and followed him. Sparks flew everywhere. Thick dust enveloped us and obscured our vision. When the air cleared, we saw that the tubs lay like a distorted pyramid, completely blocking the air-road. After a lot of effort, we righted them and cleared the area.

Peering into the gloom, Alec shouted, "Is tha all reet, Cecil?" Then again, "Weer art tha, Cecil?"

It seemed an age before we got our reply, "Course, I'm all reet. What's tha fussin' for? Nowt wrong wi' me." He emerged from his man-hole and we saw that he hadn't a scratch on him.

"Well, what does tha think abaht that?" Ted questioned, looking flabbergasted "I've known thee all this time an' all tha's ever said to me was 'Nay'. I were feelin' sorry for thee 'cos I thowt tha couldna say owt else."

"Course I can," replied Cecil, taking a long drink from his flask. "But I only gab when I've got summat decent t'talk abaht." With that, he walked past us, muttering to himself and tapping his stick.

SILENCE IS GOLDEN

Idle chit-chat was not for Paddy, no way.
All he would mutter was an 'Aye' or a 'Nay':
A man of the earth, a soul apart.
Often we wondered 'Just where do we start?'

"Evenin', Paddy, another wet neet."
Just an 'Aye' or a 'Nay', discourse complete.
"'e says 'Nay' that often an' we know 'e's more able.
Someone owt shove 'im in a stable."

Pursued by tubs, shedding their load,
Old Paddy dived headlong down an air-road.
When silence returned and the dust had cleared,
We stood in the gloom, shouted and peered.

"Art all reet, Paddy," came the cry.
'Aye, oh, Aye' was the breathless reply.
Then a grey, dusty figure emerged at last.
Could this be the Ghost of Christmas Past?

"Safe at last," we agreed with smiles.
The speed he was going, he could have travelled for miles.
"Thowt you were a goner, Paddy, me lad
But 'earin' 'Aye, oh, Aye' made us all very glad."

"Tha never says much, Paddy, except 'Aye' an' 'Nay'.
'ow about you 'avin' a bit more to say?"
"Mind thy tongue, son, or I'll give thee a clout.
I'll talk when you've got summat worth talkin' about."

Another drink from his flask. Then back up the slope.
He stopped to gaze at the broken rope.
And tapping his stick, he picked his slow way
Toward the pit-bottom and a new-born day.

D. Hollows

15. INFRA DIGNITALEM

In the darkness, away from sensitive ears, some of our colleagues could swear like the proverbial troopers. Colourful utterances would pour forth with great regularity. Pent-up emotions, frustrations, even humour, could induce a diversity of lurid language and invective. It was simply a tool to emphasise either anger or jest. This was all part of the miners' world, an accepted ritual of the underground brotherhood.

Fatigue showed on their blackened faces as they emerged from the cage into the light of day.

As they showered, those noble, unassuming and heroic men began to discard all improprieties.

The pit-gate became the back-cloth for new approaches. Expletives and profanities were consigned to the earth below. Common courtesies were accorded to all and sundry. Swearing became infra dig and especially so in front of women and children. Oaths were absorbed into the day's history. That is, until the next shift when a new chapter would begin.

INFRA DIGNITALEM

T'shift's o'er, Willie, so mind thy mouth.
Now, it's 'Please' an' 'Ta muchly', like they says down south.
Ah, 'ere comes Mrs. Smith an' 'er young kid.
"Art all reet, Mrs. an' 'ow's your Sid?"

See that smile, Willie? I said it reet
An' 'er'll be thinkin' I'm very sweet.
Oh, 'ere comes t'vicar, a real nice feller.
"'ow do, father. Regards to t'missus, tell 'er."

It's wha' they call 'manners', Willie, me lad.
Cussin' an' swearin' makes everyone sad.
Mind thee, it's 'ard keep up wi' it all t'time.
That's why I'm glad I works down in t'mine.

Mornin', Willie. I'm pleased new shift's begun.
Remember wha' I told thee abaht manners, me son?
Now I'm going t'forget mine, you thick so and so.
Tha's just dropped thy 'ammer on me b....y big toe.

16. MY MEETING WITH WINNIE

The day dawned bright and clear. My short break had begun and I was determined to enjoy the luxury of not having to go underground for a few days.

Feeling that it was much too pleasant to remain indoors, my father and I decided to go for a 'cycle ride. We left the smoky town behind us and soon we were pedalling down green, country lanes. There was a wonderful freshness all around and the air smelled so good.

After travelling for several miles, we decided to call on a relative of ours who lived in the neighbouring town of Leigh. Some years had passed since our last visit. We had kept in touch of course by letter, and we now felt that it was high time to pay our respects to cousin Clifford and his new bride.

Once arrived, we exchanged cordial greetings and were invited indoors. The exercise had made us quite hungry and with much appreciated cups of tea and biscuits, we settled down in the sitting-room and chatted away.

"How is your wife Kate?" Dad asked.

"Oh, fine," Clifford replied. "She's shopping at the moment but she shouldn't be too long. She'll be delighted to see you both." A brief silence followed as we enjoyed our refreshments.

Suddenly, from an adjoining room, came a squawky voice.

"Who is it? Who is it? What are you doing here?"

"Sounds as though Kate's back," I said. "Her throat seems to be pretty sore, poor girl."

Again, the voice screeched "What are you doing here?"

"Nice greeting," I thought "Maybe we've outstayed our welcome."

Dad and I exchanged glances. Clifford remained in his chair and looked quite unconcerned. The door opened and in walked Kate. We were amazed when a voice behind her shouted, "Where's Hitler? Bring him here. I'll soon sort him out."

Amused by the expressions on our faces, our hosts burst into laughter.

"There's your mystery voice," said Clifford and he pointed to a bird-cage in a corner of the living-room. Strutting up and down on its perch was a small, green budgerigar, looking very agitated.

"That's our Winnie," Kate smiled.

The little bird seemed to fix his eyes on me and repeated, "Where's Hitler? Bring him here. I'll soon sort him out."

Then he added, "Victory V, Victory V."

As I looked at our tiny feathered friend, I thought, "If anyone can sort out Adolf, it will surely be you, Winnie. The sooner the better."

17. HIS WONDERS TO PERFORM

The General Strike of 1926 caused untold misery for thousands of people, not least for the miners. As a child in later years, I well remember my parents and grandparents discussing that unfortunate period and telling how they had donated money to provide food and clothing to help alleviate the suffering of so many who had been caught up in the dispute.

Extreme hunger and deprivation prompted families to retire early to their beds, often by lunch-time, so that they would not expend what little energy they had. Small shop-keepers in coalfield areas extended credit to needy families to such a degree that some almost bankrupted themselves. Older miners with whom I worked gave detailed accounts of their experiences during those bleak days. As late as the 1940's, some of my colleagues were still paying off family debts on a weekly basis. Their tales of fortitude, courage and their great sense of decency in honouring their financial commitments made a deep impression on me.

The night-shift snap time arrived and I settled down with my companion who, for the sake of anonymity, I will call 'Tom'. As we ate I asked him about the strike.

"They were bad days for all of us," he said. Tom was a mine of information, very well read and a budding author. He continued, "It played havoc with my nerves, what with mounting debts, not enough food and all the attendant evils. I had my parents to care for and not a bean to my name. It got so rough that I felt I had to get right away from it all."

"What did you do, Tom, pack up and leave?" I queried.

"No, worse," he replied. "I decided to end it." He paused for a moment as if re-living old memories then he said, "I can see that you are interested and I want to tell you what happened because something weird occurred. It was about one o'clock in the morning when I finally made up my mind. It was a chill, dark night. I walked to the canal and stood there just staring into the water. At first, I hesitated but I was determined to go through with it. I was standing right on the edge of the embankment when I heard the sound of running feet on the towpath. I turned. A figure moved toward me and a voice cried, 'Don't do it, Tom. You have too much to live for.' Then again 'That's not the way, Tom. Let's talk about it'."

It was as if Tom were re-enacting the whole episode. He went on, "I turned and in the gloom I saw that it was my vicar. I asked him how he knew what I intended to do. Came the vicar's reply 'I hadn't any idea what to expect. It is all rather strange and wonderful really. I was sitting in my study preparing my sermon. The hour was late and normally I would have been in my bed. As I sat there, a warm feeling came over me. I felt drawn by some unseen force. Somehow, I knew that I had to leave my sermon half-finished and head for the canal. I did not know exactly why but I did know that I had to get there as quickly as possible. You are the answer, Tom'."

I could swear that I saw a tear run down Tom's cheek as he reminisced.

"I was amazed," said Tom. "I just couldn't understand it at all but I went to the vicarage where I was given a meal and a hot drink. That, Derek, my lad, changed my whole life. Eventually, I went back to work and now I have paid off all my debts. It's all down to a caring man and I like to think, someone else."

"Indeed," I agreed.

"And to cap it all, I have been a lay-preacher for some years and I love it," he continued. He smiled and in the dim light of our battery lamps, his face seemed to take on a radiance not of this world.

"Thank you for the story, Tom," I said. "God moves in mysterious ways," at which he nodded and smiled.

18. DEEDS NOT WORDS

Robbo wasn't a bad soul really. He would always lend a hand when called upon. Physically, he was a towering man of great strength and had an unusually ruddy complexion for a miner. Everything about him was outsize. Even his helmet seemed too small for his ample head. His abdomen, nurtured by pints of beer day in and day out, hung over his belt and swung from side to side as he walked. It gave him no end of trouble, especially when he had to crawl through a narrow fault on the face. I remember that he had a raucous laugh and unfortunately possessed a fiery temper, which always ended up in threats rather than physical violence. At least he observed the rules of underground by restraining himself.

In comparison, Billy was minute in stature. He was a sober, modest man who had little to say. The two worked together but were complete opposites.

The trouble started at snap-time. Robbo, Billy, Steve and I were about to eat our sandwiches when Robbo glared at Billy and boomed, "Any more from thee, man an' I'll sort thee out." From Billy, there was no response. It reminded me of a Laurel and Hardy scenario. Neither Steve nor I knew the reason for this outburst but I do know that we felt very uncomfortable.

Steve tugged at my sleeve and whispered, "They've been like this for months. Anyone would think they're married." At this, I laughed.

"What's up with thee?" Robbo stared hard and menacingly at me.

"Er, nothing, Robbo," I replied and averted my gaze. Had he swung his enormous girth in my direction, I would have been incapacitated.

The shift passed with occasional threats from Robbo that he would sort out Billy, sooner rather than later.

We surfaced on a bright summer's evening. We breathed deeply. The warmth of the sun felt good on our blackened faces. As we descended the steps, Steve nudged my arm. "Hey up, he's at it again," he said. I looked down into the pit-yard where a small group of spectators had assembled. True enough, Robbo had Billy by the throat and we heard him bellow "Now I'll put paid to thee once and for all."

I was amazed to see Billy make a sudden dexterous move and even more so when I saw Robbo lying flat on his back. Winded, he gasped "A' reet, Billy, let's be mates. I swear I'll never 'ave a go at thee again."

"Think he means it?" I asked Steve.

"If he doesn't now, he soon will," came the reply.

"How come?" I questioned.

"Well, I'll let you into a little secret. Not many lads in t'pit know about it."

"And what's that?" I was eager to learn.

"Billy's a judo instructor and has a part-time job training the local police. It'll make my day giving Robbo the good news," Steve smiled.

DEEDS NOT WORDS

The small one was quiet, the big one was loud:
Workmates dogged by a growing cloud.
No one knew why. It made one scared.
Only the brave might ask but no one dared.

They worked well together, like brothers-in-arms
With the big one a bully and lacking all charms.
The quiet one docile, soaking up threats,
Unmoved, unperturbed, no retaliatory steps.

Came the end of the shift and quite a surprise.
What lay before us opened our eyes.
In the yard below, two figures merged.
Cries of "Go, get 'im," both men were urged.

"Sorry, mate," groaned the loud mouth, in obvious pain,
"Friends forever, eh? No goadin' again."
It was a deft move from the tormented who was quite small
Proving the adage, "The bigger they are, the harder they fall.

D. Hollows

19. ONCE BITTEN, TWICE SHY

Steve, the collier, peered through the gloom. "I'll be reet glad to finish t'shift," he exclaimed. "Could just murder a hot cuppa n' a fag." He looked at Arnold and me, two green Bevin boys and asked, "Does tha smoke?"

"No," we answered with one accord.

Barney, the other collier, interrupted, "Tha doesna need t'smoke. Tha knows that, Steve. I don't smoke either. Prefer ma pigtail. Damn sight cheaper an' all."

"Can't stand the stuff," Steve replied.

"What's a pigtail?" Arnold asked.

Thereupon, Barney rummaged in his pocket and withdrew a small length of something we had not seen before. "This is a pigtail," he said and then bit off a chew.

"Looks like brown liquorice," I commented.

"Better than liquorice," boasted Barney. "All reet, it's good for tha bowels but this stuff is better. Gets rid of t'dust in tha mouth an' that's what we need down 'ere on t'face." Then he spat and chewed and chewed and spat with amazing regularity. Brown stains were now appearing round his lips and down his chin, a sight which made our snap-time sandwiches seem much less appealing.

"It's bacco really," Barney asserted. "Some o' t'lads use it to get over t'tobacco craving. 'Ere, try some. it'll keep tha mouth fresh."

"Tha mun be jokin'," said Steve. "Don't tempt t'lads."

His comment only served as a challenge to Arnold and myself. I expect we both wanted to fit into the scheme of things, be accepted, we felt.

Arnold and I began to chew. Soon, it became a competition between us to see who could last the longer. Arnold chewed several times, screwed up his face and hastily discarded his piece.

"Well done, Derek lad, tha's won", Barney laughed and gave me a hearty slap on the back, with disastrous results. Down went the plug and for his well-intentioned carelessness and indeed, for many hours to come, I paid the penalty. I'll choose liquorice every time.

A SALUTARY LESSON

I thought it the manly thing to do,
To mimic my elders and try out a chew.
"Keeps t'mouth moist. Gets rid o' t'dust.
So get on wi' it, lad an' chew if tha must.

Whatever tha does, don't swaller, my son.
Picks, shovels an' pigtails is 'ow coal's allus been won.
Ask any collier an' e'll tell thee that's t'truth.
Oh, tha's swallered thy plug, lad. 'ecky thump, strewth.

Tha's screwin' thy face son, Did not fancy thy treat?
Come to think on it, tha's gone white as a sheet.
Tak' my advice, boy an' when t'bad feelin' stops,
Forget all abaht pigtails an' suck acid drops."

D. Hollows

20. IGNORANCE IS BLISS

The small row of terraced houses stood but a stone's throw from the mine. They were in a state of disrepair and showed signs of subsidence. Some had been shored up with thick wooden supports. Every day, I passed them on my way to work.

On warm sunny afternoons, old Seth would sit on an empty drinks crate outside his front door and watch the world go by.

He must have been well into his eighties and looked quite frail. He was always dressed in a threadbare jacket, a muffler round his neck and a pair of clogs on his feet. When first I met him, I noticed the pallor in his cheeks, punctuated by a series of blue scars, the mark of the miner.

As I walked by, he would shout, "Afternoon, going to t'pit then?" to which I would nod in reply.

The weeks passed and I got to know him better. Very soon, we became much more communicative.

One day, he called "Has tha got a paper on thee son?"

I handed him my daily and remarked "Grand day for relaxing and having a quiet read."

"Ta," he acknowledged. "I collect 'em, tha knows."

"You must be, a mine of information," I joked.

"Oh, I don't read 'em. Don't listen to t'wireless either. I tie 'em up into a twist an' light fire with 'em," he said. Then he asked, "Come from minin' stock, does tha?"

"I believe that one of my distant relatives was a mining-engineer" I answered.

"There y' are then," he said. "It must be in tha blood." He continued, "I were a collier. So was me dad. Worked in 'Addock. Spent years on t'face. It were damned 'ard."

I looked at the towering, smouldering slag-heap behind him and pointed. "So you managed to make that on your own, did you?"

He followed my gaze. "Nay," he laughed. "But tha'd think so, all t'shovellin' I did." He went on, "Tha can't 'ave been down t'pit long cos tha's got them new safety-boots round tha neck."

"Only a few months," I told him.

He stared at my steel, toe-capped footwear and asked, "Weer did tha get them posh boots from then?"

"The Government" I replied.

"The Government?" he repeated. "What the 'ells come o' er 'em, givin' boots away? They should've given thee clogs. A lot cheaper."

"Well," I advised. "We all got them. We were balloted, you know."

Seth bit off a chew from his pigtail. "Go on," he urged. "Sounds very interestin'. Who balloted thee then?"

"Mr. Bevin," I responded.

His face took on a puzzled expression. Scratching his head, he said, "I must say I've 'eard o' Chamberlain an' o' Winnie Churchill but Bevin. Let me think." He pondered awhile. "Nay," he said. "Don't know 'im." He looked at me and asked, "Who the b★★★dy 'ell's Bevin?"

BLACK MOUNTAIN (THE SLAG-HEAP)

The black mountain rises, kissing the sky,
Smouldering, smoking, as we pass by.
A furnace that speaks of the labours of man,
A reminder of toil since the mine began.

No birds here to sing and to fly,
O' er the black mountain that kisses the sky.
Much pain lies there, recorded in flames,
A burning list of countless names.

'Tis said things change with the passing of days
And wonders are ceaseless in so many ways.
Pray Nature's fruits may soon be seen
And the black mountain emerges a living green.

D. Hollows

21. THE COST OF COAL

The cage surfaced and out stepped a small group of miners. Their faces, masked by coaldust, looked gaunt. Between them, they carried a stretcher on which lay a still form. Reverently, they bore it down the steps to the waiting ambulance.

I watched them as they handed it over so gently to the crew and with one last look, they turned and slowly walked toward the Manager's office. They looked spent and dejected and I felt sorry for them.

After the customary search for cigarettes, matches and lighters, I took my turn in the queue.

"What's happened?" someone asked.

The banksman whispered, "Been crushed between t'tubs. Not yet seventeen an' he's dead."

Suddenly, from behind us, there came a dreadful scream. With one accord, we turned to identify the source and saw a newly-arrived Bevin Boy.

"I can't go down there," he sobbed. "I just can't. I hate being shut in. Can't breathe. Don't care what they do to me. I'm not going down. His face was ashen, sweat poured from his brow and his whole frame was shaking uncontrollably. He was in an extreme state of hysteria.

"Pity someone 'adn't sense t'sort him out afore. Would 'ave saved the lad a lot o' grief," a collier commented.

One of my colleagues put a fatherly arm round the boy's shoulder and spoke to him gently and reassuringly, "Tha'll be a'reet, son. Dunna be afeared. We'll look after thee."

It was all to no avail. The youngster broke free, shouting, "I can't go down there. I'm too frightened." With that, he ran down the steps and across the pit-yard. We never saw him again but we all fervently hoped that he would be treated with a great deal of understanding and compassion.

Deep in thought, we entered the cage. The bell rang.

"Bloody, bloody war," exclaimed one of the men. Then we plunged into the depths.

EPITAPH FOR A LOST BOY
(In memory of a teenager killed underground, Lyme Colliery, 1945).

His day is done in a darkened mine
But from those depths, a light will shine
On a tender youth with a spirit sweet
Now resting at our Saviour's feet.

God's great Mercy grants pain's release.
After toil and labour comes blessed Peace.
So dry your tears and live each day
And give thanks unto the Lord, I pray.

The sun will smile and breezes blow,
From which will come the warming glow
Of a caring soul who stands close by.
True love is eternal. It does not die.

From azure skies far up above.
O' er kith and kin, he'll shed that love.
Freed at last from earthly strife.
There is no death. 'tis Higher Life.

D. Hollows

22. MON PETIT VOCABULAIRE

For two years, I had been studying French at my local Grammar School. I was hopeless at science subjects, especially chemistry but I thoroughly enjoyed English, French and Latin, at which I felt that I was a reasonable performer.

One evening, there was a knock at our front door, which my father answered. "A lady is asking for you," he said. "She appears to be very excited and she is waiting in the sitting-room." I saw that she was a near neighbour of ours whose husband, a navigator, had been reported "missing in action."

"You study French at school, don't you, Derek?" she said. "I don't know where this letter's come from but it was pushed through my letter-box this morning. It wasn't stamped. It's addressed to me and it's written in French. Can you help me?"

"This is exciting," I thought. "Straight out of 'Adventure' and 'Rover' comics." I believe that I translated the letter to her satisfaction. It appeared that her husband had been shot down over South-East Belgium and that he was safe and well. Because of injuries to his hands, he was unable to write himself. A group of Resistance fighters were caring for him in the Ardennes region. Apologies were offered for the fact that none of the group could write in English.

To think that I had seen and handled an item from Occupied Europe prompted me to intensify my language studies and I was determined that, at some time in the future, I would become fluent. Truth to tell, that came many years later.

Before reporting for my post-training Bevin Boy duties, I made a point of securing a pocketsize copy of 'Petit Vocabulaire', a book which I had used at school. I vowed to study it at every available opportunity, especially during slack periods when I operated a nine inch haulage machine and at snap-times.

"Wha's tha readin'?" Paddy asked, peering over my shoulder. "Oh, it's a foreign language, ain't it? Man, tha mun be bright. How many languages can'st speak then?"

"Well, there's English," I replied.

"Aye, so I've noticed," he said.

"And I've done some Latin."

"Wha's that?" he questioned.

"Its a language used very rarely nowadays and it was spoken by the Romans many years ago. Then, of course, there's French." Paddy was counting on his fingers. "That mak's three," he observed and added, "An if tha stops down 'ere long enough, tha'll speak four."

"How come?" I asked.

"Well," he asserted proudly, "There's Yicker."

"What's that?" I queried.

"It's t'language we speak in 'Addock" and off he went.

I took great care of that little book. It never went out of my sight until one day, we had a build-up of gas. Air pipes were brought in to clear it. I'd left my book by my machine. Just as the 'All Clear' was given and we prepared to resume work, there was a heavy roof-fall and that little companion of mine was completely buried. Even if retrieved from under that mountain of rubble, it would have been irreparably damaged.

Occasionally, I think back to that time and wonder what really became of it. We were often visited by our furry friends, the mice who boldly faced us waiting for tit-bits. They would find anything, anywhere.

The mine closed down many years ago. I often wonder if I might have left a legacy shared by several generations of bi-lingual mice who communicated in Yicker and French. It's a thought.

And what became of the navigator? He was taken prisoner and returned safely home at the end of the war.

MON PETIT VOCABULAIRE

That little blue book was my bosom friend,
A bond that I felt would never end.
The words therein oft spoke to me,
Even underground when 'twas hard to see.

La langue Francaise my daily pleasure
And fluency grew beyond all measure.
I must admit the sciences were never my forte.
So no interest, no effort, very naughty.

The tunnel is sealed. The gas is cleared,
A minor crisis and less than we feared.
Then comes the thunder of groaning rock
As Mother Earth reels in sudden shock.

For my entombed book I felt so sad
But in retrospect, maybe, it wasn't so bad.
Comes solace from that crumbling kench
Enabling 'Yicker' mice to speak in French.

D. Hollows

23. REVERIE

That night, at snap-time, I sat in a man-hole and ate alone. Barney and Steve were shoring up and unable to join me. Apart from the occasional tapping of a hammer, there was silence.

"Not the same without them," I thought. "No one to talk to. Won't be sorry when this break's over."

Came a voice from the darkness. "Hi, friend, enjoying your grub? Got a bite for me?"

I jumped up and looked round. Not a soul to be seen. Again the voice spoke, "Don't eat it all, pal. I'm starving." The hair on the back of my neck bristled and in spite of the intense heat, I felt a shiver run down my spine.

"All the mines in Lancashire and I've landed up in one that's haunted," I murmured. "Who's there? Show yourself," I shouted.

"I'm here, mate. Here I am, down here," the words came from around my feet.

I looked down and was amazed to see a little grey mouse, staring up at me. "Not possible," I determined. He wore a helmet with its battery-lamp and carried a stick. Strangest of all, he wore tiny clogs. He placed his oil-lamp down beside him and said,

"That's it. Now you know where I am."

"What the......," I exclaimed but he interrupted me.

"You're a Bevin Boy, I can tell. You've got those new boots on. If you want to know anything about this pit, just ask me or one of my cousins. We've been down here for ages and we know everything that's going on."

"Your cousins?" I asked. "How many are there?"

"Oh, hundreds," he declared. "Let's have a nibble of your sandwich and I'll tell you all about it. I'm really famished."

He sat down next to me in the man-hole. I broke off a piece of bread and gave it to him, He had an enormous appetite. There was complete silence until he'd finished off the contents of my snap-tin.

"That's better. Thanks, mate," he said. He burped, yawned, stretched and scratched himself, then looked at me.

"Got a name?" I asked.

"Of course, I have. It's Montague, Monty to my friends," he replied.

"Often get hungry?" I queried.

"Sure do, but most of the lads throw us tasty bits. Mind you, sometimes we pinch it."

"What do you mean, pinch it?" I questioned.

He turned his head to the left, then to the right, as if looking for eavesdroppers. Satisfied, he whispered, "Some of the chaps came down here without snap-tins. Not many, mind you. They hide it in their jacket pockets and leave them lying about. Bevin Boys are the worst. My buddy, Charlie, keeps a sharp look-out and then we strike. Others tie fuse-wire round their food parcels and fasten them to an arch. Think we can't get at them but there's no stopping us. As far as we're concerned, they could put axle grease on the wire. It wouldn't make a scrap of difference."

"I know," I agreed. "It happened to me only last week. Even took the paper."

"We like paper too," he answered. "Makes our homes nice and cosy. It it's got a pattern on it, we do a bit of wallpapering. We've got some very nice houses down here."

"So you live in a little village then?"

"A village?" he repeated in an admonishing tone. "Why it's bigger than Haydock and Earlestown put together. Of course, most of the properties belong to my cousins. I've got relations living down Wood Pit and Boston. In fact, they're all over the place, even in Ashton and Golborne. One or two reckon they may be selling up in a few years."

"Why, where are they thinking of going?" I asked.

"They've been talking about buying luxury flats in that new Winwick Colliery Development when it's ready," he said.

I had warmed to my new-found friend. "How on earth did you get down here?" I was anxious to know.

"I was born down here," came the reply. "My great, great, great grandad settled here first. I'm not sure how he got down the shaft though." He scratched his ear and went on, "Have you ever read a book called 'The Road to Wigan Pier', by a chap called Orwell?"

I nodded.

"It's a brilliant book. Tells you a lot about the miners and he even mentions us," Monty continued. "When I was a nipper and tucked up in bed, my mum used to take it off the shelf and read me bedtime stories from it. George said that my ancestors might possibly have got down here by falling down the shaft."

"Not likely," I interrupted. "They'd have been flattened."

"Sorry to contradict you," Monty said. "If you know anything about mice, you'd realise that their surface area is very large relative to their weight. Oh, yes, we know how to land on our feet all right."

"There must have been an easier way," I suggested.

"Agreed," he responded. "Most of them went down in the straw with the ponies, no doubt. Knowing my relatives as I do, I'd say that they preferred to travel in comfort. They're a bit toffee-nosed, you know and only first-class would do."

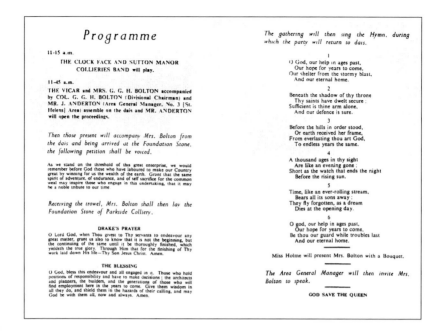

The official programme of the opening of Parkside Colliery (Mr. Simm).

"You have quite an intellect, Monty," I commented. "You should write a book about us humans."

"No books, no time to do it," he answered. "It's a full-time job looking after our mates."

"What do you mean, looking after them?"

"Well, it's favour for favour really. They give us tit-bits and to show our appreciation, we give them our support. I'll let you into a little secret. When the ground starts to shake, we can feel it well before they do. Sometimes, it's miles off but we know what's coming. So my pals and I run to and fro in front of them and just to make sure that they've noticed us, we do a little jig. Then we dive for cover and so do they." Monty's voice seemed to fade into a whisper.

There was a sharp tug at my sleeve, followed by another. "Come on, Dek lad. Snaptimes o' er. Tha's been fast asleep." Drowsily, I looked up to see Barney's face.

POSTSCRIPT

The new Winwick Development to which Monty referred later became known as Parkside Colliery.

24. MINING HUMOUR (Recorded in the 40's)

The bond between miners throughout the world is unique. This relationship has been forged through their cognizance of the dangers which beset all who work underground.

The wit of the miner is legendary and has been revealed in many tongues and a variety of dialects.

Here, in our own coalfields, it was never expressed in a derogatory manner at the expense of the Bevin Boy. Rather, the latter was the foil who became an integral part of that discourse. Without him, many classic expressions may have lain dormant, perhaps even, non-existent.

To men and boys engaged in onerous and perilous duties, good-natured chit-chat formed a part of their daily routine and served as a salve to help ease the stresses of their tasks.

Over sixty years ago, Bevin Boys witnessed countless incidents of humorous exchanges which they still recall with clarity.

"Snap Time." A time for rest, replenishment and witty conversation.

I find it nostalgic for me to include some examples of that wit which I recorded during my period of service.

25. DIALECT HUMOUR

Short cut

"Tha's got a terrible limp. What's up with thee?" asked Elwyn.

"It's me toe-nails," Archie replied.

"What's up with 'em?"

"They've grown that long, I can 'ardly get me clogs on."

"Why don't tha cut em with t'scissors?"

"Lost 'em."

"Has tha tried a file?"

"Lost that an' all."

"What abaht goin' to t'farrier?"

"I ain't daft. Think I want t'hurt mysen?"

"Tell thee what," said Elwyn.

"When t'shift's o' er, we'll trim 'em wi' t'coal-cutter."

"Now tha's talkin'," replied Archie.

Enough is enough

Joe took off his clogs and socks and rubbed his aching feet.

"By gum, thy socks don't 'alf pong," said Fred. "'ow often does tha wash 'em?"

"Every day," came the reply.

"Tha's a reet liar," laughed Fred.

"True as I sit 'ere," said Joe, looking around. Then he exclaimed.

"Me socks 'as gone. Has tha seen 'em?"

"Aye," replied Fred. "Better get movin'. They've jus' walked off down th' aulage-road."

Close call

With blackened faces, the collier and the pit-brow lass gazed at each other across the canteen.

"Ee, but tha'll be reet fair when tha gets that muck off thy face," the collier shouted.

"So will thee," replied the lass.

"Wan't t'go to t'flicks toneet?" he asked.

"Aye," she answered.

"Meet thee outside t'Palace at seven then?" he said.

"Reet. Sithee," she agreed.

Promptly at seven, they arrived outside the cinema. The collier walked toward the lass.

"By the 'eck, what's tha doin' 'ere, Grannie?" he asked.

"Gorra date wi' a collier," she replied.

Life's a drag

"Did tha notice that woman in t'canteen?" Tommy asked at snap time.

"Should 'ave. I were standin' reet next to thee," Gus replied.

"She were smokin' a fag while she were butterin' t'bread,"

Tommy went on. "There were an inch of ash on that ciggie."

"Aye, I noticed that," Gus agreed.

"Just as she were spreadin' t'jam on, it fell reet off an' into t'butties. That's why I didn't get me snap today," Tommy said.

"Wonder what 'appened to them butties?" Gus mused.

"Tha's just eaten 'em," Tommy replied.

Not always in threes

"Joe's been 'avin' a rough time of it lately," said Griff.

"Why so?" asked the Bevin Boy.

"Well, for starters, 'is lad's got ringworm. 'is missus 'as got death-watch beetle in 'er wooden leg an' 'e's got woodworm in 'is furniture."

"Could be worse, I suppose," said the Bevin Boy.

"'appen not," Griff replied. "T'cap it all, poor chap's got dry rot an' wet rot."

"Not surprising," said the Bevin Boy. "I've always said it's too damned hot down here. Damp and all."

Class act

"Pass us some o' them props," said Bert to the Bevin Boy.

"Do you want Aladdin's lamp, Widow Twanky's outfit or the back end of a pantomime cow?"

"What the 'ell's drivellin' on abaht?" asked Bert.

"Before I came down here, I was a stage-hand," the boy replied.

Not ready yet

It was practice night for the miners' brass-band.

"Reet, lads, tune up," said the bandmaster. Looking round, he asked,

"Weer's Willie wi' 'is cornet?"

"Be 'ere soon," said Sam.

"Why, is 'e in t'toilet then?"

"Nay, 'e's eatin' it."

Creature comforts

"It's a long way to the workings. I'm shattered," moaned the Bevin Boy.

"So tha's not 'eard then?" asked Charlie.

"Heard what?"

"Come Monday, they're runnin' a bus service from t'pit-bottom."

Bright idea

It was change of shift time. As they surfaced, the collier looked at the Bevin Boy and asked,

"Does tha like board-games?"

"Sure do," the lad replied.

The collier looked round at his work-mates and started counting.

"What are you doing?" queried the Bevin Boy.

"Just seein' if there's enough for a game o' draughts," the miner said.

Patience is a virtue

The Bevin Boy stepped into the cage for the first time.

"How long does it take to reach the bottom?" he asked.

"Not long," came the reply.

"I want to get it over and done with," the boy said nervously.

"Well, if tha jumps down t'shaft instead o' travellin' in t'cage, it will be," the miner observed.

Ill-prepared

"I'm sick o' t'ruddy blackout," said Henry at snap-time.

"Me, too," Willie replied. "It's 'ard gettin' used to t'dark."

Sacrifice

"Not 'ad a proper 'ot meal for a week," Ted moaned.

"Why, doesn't thy missus cook for thee?"

"'er can't."

"Can't cook?"

"Well, really 'er can but now 'er can't."

"How does't mean?"

"'er's given all t'pots an' pans to t'Spitfire Fund."

Substitute

"I see Barney's joined th'ome Guard but 'e's not very 'appy."

"Why not?"

"Cos 'e ain't got a gun yet. Mind thee, I don't know what 'e's complainin' about. 'e's got a uniform an' a brush."

"Tha can't fight wi' a brush."

"It's not for fightin' wi'."

"What then?"

"They've given 'im t'job o' sweepin' up t'Drill 'all."

Crossed–wires

"Tha's late gettin' on t'face, Tommy. Weer's tha been?"

"Eh, wha's that?" "I said,

"Weer's tha been? Art deaf, lad?"

"Am I 'eck. 'ad me ears syringed las' Tuesday."

"Well then, answer me question. Weer's tha been?"

"Oh, aye. 'er were on t'wireless las' neet."

"Who were?"

"Why, Vera Lynn."

Exclusive membership

"Lancashire miners are called 'Cloggies', tha knows," said Arthur.

"I'm a Lancashire lad, born and bred, so I'm a Cloggie then?" asked the Bevin Boy.

"No chance," Arthur advised.

"Why not?"

"Cos tha's wearin' them new boots owd Bevin gave thee," came the reply.

Made it

"This gradient's very steep," said the Bevin Boy.

"Takes you all your time to walk up it."

"Better up it than down it. Safer an' all," Harry replied.

"How do you mean, 'safer'?" the Bevin Boy asked.

"Well, ten year ago, owd Sammy ran down it."

"What happened?"

"'e couldn't stop runnin' an' 'e went straight down th'air road."

"Did you find him?"

"Nay, lad, but I got a card from 'im last week."

"Where from?"

"Australia."

Mass produced

"'ow many lads does think Bevin's got down t'pit now?" asked Ebenezer.

"Should think there's a few thousand and there'll be more to come," the Bevin Boy replied.

"Tha don't say. I feel reet sorry for 'is missus. 'er mun be fair wore out," observed Ebenezer.

'er's not daft

"That Charlie's missus is a reet un," said Eli.

"Aye, 'er's been round t'block a few times," added Josh.

"What do you mean?" asked the Bevin Boy.

"Every pay-day 'er waits at t'gate for 'is wages," Eli answered.

"Maybe she can't trust him," suggested the Bevin Boy.

"'er don't trust no one. That's why 'er collects Tommy's, Zak's an' Ezra's an' all," Eli replied.

"Why theirs?" the Bevin Boy queried.

"Like I said afore, 'er's been round t'block a few times an' 'er's got fourteen kids t'feed," replied Josh.

A fishy tale

"'ow is it that every time Merv comes off t'shift, 'e comes back soakin' wet an' wi' a load o' mackerel?" asked Job.

"That's easy. It's cos t'face 'e's workin' on's under t'North Sea," Teddy replied.

What a liberty

"Sorry t'tell thee but mice 'ave just eaten thy butties," said Luther to Henry.

"Tha's what comes o' not usin' thy snap-tin," Gordon interrupted.

"Nay, can't be my grub. I know I put it in me tin," Henry insisted.

"So tha did," said Luther. Trouble is, I forgot mine so I borrowed thine. Mind thee, I took care t'take thy butties out first."

Black ice

"Believe tha 'ad a spot o' bother last neet, Billy," said Hughie.

"Did an' all," Billy replied. "I were ridin' 'ome on me bike an' I went slap-bang into th'ice-cream chap. Tha knows, the one wi' 'Stop me an' buy one' on 'is box."

"Wha' did 'e say?" asked Hughie.

"Not much but 'e were real angry wi' me," came the reply.

"So tha stopped 'im an' bought one, I see," Hughie observed.

"Tha can say that again," Billy answered, fingering his black eye.

Problem solved

During his pre-underground training, a Bevin Boy was assigned to the screening-plant.

"Tha looks awful. What's up with thee?" queried a pit-brow lass.

"Terrible toothache. Any dentists round here?" he asked.

"Oh, aye," came the reply. "There's one opposite t'Town 'all."

"Thanks. Good at his job, is he?" questioned the anxious boy.

"Owt to be," came the response. "Afore 'e set up in teeth, 'e were a ripper down t'pit."

"Don't think I'll bother today," said the Bevin Boy. "The pain's just gone."

One stood alone

Invariably, at snap-time, Tommy ate cheese and pickled-onion sandwiches... He had but one tooth in his head, a chewing-tobacco stained canine.

"Why don't tha get it pulled, Tommy, lad?" asked Henry.

"It looks lonely on its own."

"No chance," snarled Tommy.

"That's me pickle-stabber an' it's stayin' weer it is."

Fund-raising

Charlie the collier and the Bevin Boy walked into the packed local pub. The boy stared in amazement at the customers.

"Why are they kicking one another up the back-side. Have they all gone mad?" he asked.

"Nay, lad," Charlie replied.

"It were t'landlord's idea to 'ave a swear-box on t'counter. It's for t'miners' welfare, tha knows."

Stiff as a board

"Look at poor 'orace tryin' t'lift that there tub back on t'rails. Must be in agony. 'e can 'ardly bend," observed Sammy.

"An' that's what thirty years down t'pit does to thy back," said Pete.

"Tha can blame 'is missus," Billy advised. "Nowt t'do wi' t'pit,"

"Blame 'is missus for a bad back?" Sammy repeated.

"Bad back, me foot," Billy replied.

"'er puts too much starch in t'washin'."

Under orders

"See them bits o' rock o' er theer?"

"Yes," said the Bevin Boy.

"Well, get me shovel an' chuck it into t'tub."

"Right," answered the Bevin Boy and set about his task.

"I'll leave thee to it, lad," said the miner and off he went. Half an hour later, he returned.

"Tha's done well, son, but tha's left a bit. Pass me shovel an' I'll finish it off."

"Chucked it in the tub, as you said," replied the Bevin Boy.

"It's under all that rock."

Mickey drippin'

"Better get movin'," said Mickey.

"There's all water runnin' down me back."

"Stop frettin' lad, Henry replied.

"Just 'old on to that prop while I shore up t'roof."

"But it's gettin' worse," moaned Mickey.

"Could be in for a reet floodin', tha knows."

"What the 'ell's up wi' thee?" asked Henry, looking down at him.

"It's only sweat runnin' off me face."

Home comforts

"I hate my pit," said the Bevin Boy.

"I've got more lumps and bumps than soft Mick."

"Well, what does tha expect? Tha's bound t'get lumps an' bumps down 'ere," Jimmy replied.

"'e don't mean down 'ere," Sammy advised.

"'e's talkin' abaht 'is bed in th'ostel."

Mixed messages

"Bet thee two bob my pigeon's better than thine," said Willie.

"Reet, tha's on. Bring it to t'pit in t'mornin' an' we'll soon find out," Harry replied. The next day, both turned up for work. Harry brought his bird and Willie brought a pie.

Minor incident

Two Bevin Boys walked into the local bar.

"A pint each for a couple of parched miners, please landlord," said one.

"Minors, art tha?" the landlord queried.

"That is correct, sir."

"Well, if tha's minors, clear off. No under-age drinkin' in my pub. Tha'll get me in trouble wi' t'police."

Waste not, want not

"Ee, I'll 'ave t'get rid o' me bunions," Curly complained.

"Eh, what did tha say?" asked Dickie, cupping his ear.

"I said I'll 'ave t'get rid o' me bunions," Curly repeated.

"Oh, aye, when tha does, gie 'em to us," said Dickie.

"What the 'ell for?" asked Curly.

"Mun waste good grub. 'appen they'll go down a treat wi' me cheese butties. There's nowt like taste o' a good 'omegrown bunion straight from t'garden," Dickie replied.

How low can one get?

"Look at those mice," the Bevin Boy exclaimed.

"One's got his head bandaged, one's got his leg in plaster and all the others have got bandy legs."

"Tha'swha' comes o' workin' on a low face," Archie replied.

The beautiful game

"Last neet were a real tragedy," said Albert.

"Wha' does't mean?" asked Danny.

"Our footie-team got 'ammered."

"Who by?"

"T'Bevin Boys from th'ostel."

"Wha' were t'score?"

"Ninety-nil."

"Never."

"True as I stand 'ere."

"But we got t'best team for miles around."

"Aye, I know that but all t'lads was workin'. Only t'goalie could make it."

What goes round

Billy turned to Tommy. "Eh, lad, look o' er yon. Does think that chap couplin' t'tubs looks a dead ringer for Ernie Bevin?" he pointed.

"That's reet. It is Ernie Bevin," Tommy replied.

"Wha' the 'ell's 'e doin' down 'ere?" Billy asked.

"Resigned from t'Government an' drew 'is own number out 'is 'at," advised Tommy.

Speech therapy

Noah and Monty were working on the coalface. "By gum, I could do wi' some more air," said Noah.

"Why, art 'avin' trouble wi' thy breathin'?" asked Monty.

"Nay, I mean on me 'ead," Noah replied.

Tactful

"Hi, Tommy, not seen you for a few days. Enjoy your break?" asked the Bevin Boy.

"Not at a'," came the reply.

"Why ever not?" questioned the Boy as he autographed Tommy's plaster-cast leg.

Green fingers

Ashley looked at the Bevin Boy. "I'm 'avin' nowt but trouble wi' me kidneys. Shall 'ave t'do summat abaht it soon," he said.

"If I were you, I'd get straight round to the doctor's," advised the Bevin Boy.

"Why, does 'e grow beans an' all?" asked Ashley.

Running amok

"What does think o' t'grub in t'canteen?" asked Lol.

"Not bad at all," Mike replied.

"Don't know 'ow tha can say that," said Lol.

"Why not?"

"Didn't tha see it fall out o' t'lettuce. Afore tha knows it there'll be 'undreds of 'em all o' er t'place," Lol answered.

Good deed for the day

The cage began its descent.

"Hell, I've just lost me false-teeth," shouted Henry.

"Weer did tha lose 'em?" Toby asked.

"They fell through t'gate an' reet down t'shaft. Now, I won't be able t'eat me butties at snap-time," Henry moaned.

"Not to worry, owd lad. Tha can borrow mine," said Toby.

Calm down

Gordon, the Bevin Boy was late for his shift. He charged into the changing-room looking hot and flustered.

"The bus didn't turn up. I've run all the way here," he gasped.

"Take it easy, son," Tom reassured him.

"Don't know what's wrong but I'm having a right struggle getting these new safety-boots on, Maybe my feet are swollen with all that running," Gordon complained.

"Might be a good idea if tha takes off thy shoes first," Tom suggested.

Alternative medicine

"If tha's all blocked up an' it's drivin' thee whacky, Go to t'canteen an' get a pigtail o' baccy. When swallowed, it's good for thy innards, they say, But don't blame me if tha's on t'lavvie all day."

Sabotage

The lads were working several miles in. Ted, the deputy, arrived.

"Will tha sort this out?" said Jimmy.

"We was diggin' an' we met this bloke comin' t'other way," added Henry.

"Wha's the trouble?" asked Ted.

"Says it's 'is coal an' 'e's goin' t'sue us for pinchin' it," Jimmy replied.

"Reet," said Ted. "We'll go up to t'manager's office and let 'im deal wi' it."

"Before I can sort this out, I'll need some particulars," advised the manager. "Names, please."

"Jimmy Wicks an' 'enry Stubbs," the deputy said.

Looking up, the manager addressed the plaintiff, "And your name please?"

"Mein name is Adolf but mein friends called me 'Der Fuhrer'," came the reply. "And I vant mein coal back."

Could be worse

"It's too damned hot down here," complained the Bevin Boy.

"It's like being in hell."

"Th'only time tha needs t'worry, son," said Arnie.

"Is when tha starts t'grow a couple o' 'orns."

Poultry argument

"I'm fair famished," declared Rolf.

"Could murder a chicken buttie."

"Better duck," said Freddie.

"I said 'Chicken'," Rolf repeated.

"Duck," came the reply.

"Chicken," Rolf argued.

"Why does't keep sayin' 'duck'?"

"Cos t'roof's abaht t'come in," Freddie warned.

Geneva Convention

"'ow's that brother o'thine in Burma?" Billy asked.

"Doin' all reet," Dave replied. "Caught a Jap soldier t'other week an' marched 'im off to 'eadquarters."

"Good for 'im," said Billy.

"Thing is, when t'Jap were captured, all 'e could say were, 'ah so, ah so'." Dave added.

"Cheeky swine," Billy observed. "Your kid should of booted 'im reet up it."

Amateur meteorologist

It was a bleak, miserable day. The cage surfaced and out stepped a newly-arrived Bevin Boy from the South. Looking out over the saturated pit-yard, he asked, "Does it always rain in the North?"

"Nay, lad, only when it's wet," came the reply.

Sample the waters

"By gum, got a reet thirst on me," said Wally. "Run clean out o' water, an' all. Can spare us a sip?"

"Aye, get that there flask an' 'elp thysen," Teddy pointed.

"Ee, but it's good," Wally exclaimed. "Mind thee, this orange-juice could do wi' some more sugar in it."

"Orange-juice?" Teddy repeated.

"Silly devil, tha's picked up t'wrong flask. I'm off for a check-up at t'doctor's toneet an' tha's polished off me sample."

Fashion sense

"Does't know weer I can get some red paint?"

"Why?"

"T'missus wants 'er gas-mask t'match 'er 'air."

Wrong chap

"'ad a visitor last neet," said Archie.

"Who were it?" asked Ben.

"Jerry."

"Not Jerry. Ain't seen the ol' devil in years. 'ow were 'e?"

"Didn't ask 'im."

"Why not?"

"'e were up in t'sky droppin' bombs."

Gymnastics

Henry was walking from the lamp-room when he saw a head protruding from the surface of the pit-yard.

"What the 'ell art doin' theer, Billy?" he asked, looking down at the head.

"Weer's the rest o' thee?"

"'angin' on to me 'ead," came the reply.

"'ow did tha get like that then?"

"I were jumpin' up an' down on t'conveyor."

"Tha's warned not t'ride on t'belts. 'appen tha's jumped too 'ard."

Repetition

"'ear tha's 'ad a bit o' 'ard luck, Tommy."

"Aye, tha can say that again."

"Believe tha's 'ad a bit o' 'ard luck, Tommy. Now I've said it again, wha' more does tha want?"

Ingenious

"Wha's up wi' thee. Gorra reet miserable face?"

"Dog's chewed up me ration-book."

"Tha's nowt, lad, when tha takes it for a walk toneet, make sure tha's gorra bag 'andy an' when tha gets 'ome, that'll only need a tube o' glue."

Don't push your luck

Old Henry's leg was trapped under a tub.

"Quick, get t'doctor," shouted the pit-brow lass.

"Stop thy fussin', no need," said Henry as he unscrewed it and stood up. Promptly, he fell flat on his face, and knocked himself out.

"Quick, get t'doctor," shouted the lass. "I can't unscrew 'is 'ead."

Panic stations

"Went t'pictures wi' t'missus yesterday."

"Enjoy it?"

"Not really. When we come out, it were rainin' like mad an' I 'ad t'rush 'er off to t'doctor's."

"Why?"

"'er legs went a funny colour. Give me a reet turn it did."

"What did t'doctor say?"

"Don't go out on a wet neet wi' gravy-brownin' on thy legs."

Home comforts

"Nowt like a good bath in front o' t'fire," said Nosher.

"You mean, you don't use the showers on top?" asked the Bevin Boy.

"Nay, don't use t'bath at 'ome neither."

"Why ever not?"

"Keep me ducks in it."

Read the instructions

"Can't get the 'ang o' that dried egg stuff," said Ossie.

"Keeps fallin' through me fork."

"Tha's not doin' it reet," said Albert.

"Tha's better suckin' it through a straw, then tha don't waste it."

Wrong sort

"I've heard you've got fossils down here," said the Bevin Boy.

"Aye, that's reet, loads on 'em," Chippie replied.

"Where are they?" asked the boy.

"Look, o'er theer," Chippie pointed.

"At t'moment, they're 'avin' their snap. There's 'enry an' owd Willie. That's two for starters."

Ear, ear

"My helmet feels too tight," complained the Bevin Boy.

"Not surprised," Barnaby replied.

"I grant thee, it's freezin' on top but tha shouldn't come down t'pit wearin' them ear-muffs."

A prophecy

"It's as black as night down here," said the Bevin Boy.

"So it is," Titus answered.

"An' wouldst believe it, we've got stars an' all."

"You mean, famous people?" asked the Bevin Boy.

"Nay, lad, stars like tha' gets in t'sky at neet."

"I haven't seen any," remarked the Bevin Boy.

"Well, tha will be doin' if tha doesn't duck thy 'ead," Titus replied.

A good neighbour

"Ever 'ad one of them big tins o' jam? Come from South Africa, tha knows. My missus got one this mornin', an 'er put it on me bread for breakfast," Benjie said.

"Aye, we got a tin an' a' but t'wife won't touch the stuff," came the reply.

"Why not?" inquired Benjie. "It were reet tasty."

"She let Grandad open t'can an' 'is glass eye fell straight into t'jam. 'e were that shocked he opened 'is mouth an' 'is false teeth fell in an' all."

"Did 'er find 'em?" asked Benjie.

"Nay, 'er didn't bother lookin'."

"That mun 'ave been a shock. What did 'er do?"

"Put t'lid back on an' gave it to thy missus."

A miner's lament

There were tears in Lol's eyes as he kept repeating, "A week at t'most an'there's nowt I can do for thee."

"Wha's up, lad?" asked Percy.

"'ear tha went t'doctors last neet."

"Aye."

"News not so good then?"

"Oh, aye, nowt wrong wi' me."

"Well, why does tha keep sayin', 'A week at t'most an' there's nowt I can do for thee'?"

"I'm talkin' about me shovel. It's buggered," Lol replied.

Nothing new

"Has tha worked in t'dark afore?" asked the miner.

"Oh, aye," replied the newly-arrived local Bevin Boy.

"When were that then?" queried the miner.

"When I were at school an' couldn't do me algebra," the lad replied.

Sweet tooth

"Hey, Tommy, there's a chap down here with a load of sherbet fountains. Fancy one? I'm buying," said the Bevin Boy.

"Aye, all reet," Tommy replied.

"I'll have two please," said the Bevin Boy. "How much are they?"

"Depends," came the reply.

"Depends on what?" asked the Bevin Boy.

"Depends on whether tha wants 'em wi' or wi'out detonators," answered the shot-firer.

A clean break

"I believe owd Tom from t'lamp-room went on 'oliday last week," said Chuck.

"So 'e did. Went into t'country, bird watchin'. That's 'is 'obby, tha knows," Barney replied.

"Enjoy it, did 'e?" asked Chuck.

"Not really," came the reply " 'is wooden leg snapped off."

"'ow did that 'appen?" asked Chuck.

"A woodpecker got 'im."

Wrong address

"Our knocker-up 'ad to pack in 'is job last week," announced Albert.

"Why, what's up wi' 'im?" asked Spud.

"Got a terrible cold an' a bump as big as a coconut on 'is 'ead."

"That sounds bad. 'ow did he get it?"

"Knocked at t'wrong winder at fourin t'mornin'. T'chap went mad and threw a chamber-pot at 'im."

Hole in one

"I see 'enry's been ferretin' again," said Tommy.

"How do you know?" asked the Bevin Boy.

"Cos 'e keeps rubbin' 'is leg and sayin' 'Ooh, aah'."

"What's that got to do with it?" the Bevin Boy queried.

"Didn't tha know 'enry's short-sighted?"

"No," came the reply.

"'e keeps puttin' t'ferret down t'wrong 'ole. 'bout time 'is missus stitched up 'is trouser pockets."

It's all in the swing

"Ever played golf?" asked the Bevin Boy.

"Aye, once," Henry replied. "Enjoy it?"

"Nay, spent more time in t'trees than t'squirrels."

Room for one more

"My Grannie's proper upset and she's nearly ninety," declared the Bevin Boy.

"'ow so?" asked Wimpy.

"Well, she's no coal left in the shed and it's the middle of winter."

"Soon sorted, son," said Wimpy.

"How?" came the question.

"Tell 'er t'write to owd Bevin."

"What for? He won't give' her any coal."

"Nay, but 'e could fix it for 'er to be a volunteer."

"What, at her age?"

"Nowt t'lose, lad. 'er'll get extra grub an' clothin' coupons an' er'll be able spend most o' t'day down 'ere weer it's cosy."

"An' 'er'll 'ave an oil-lamp t'keep 'er 'ands warm," added Patrick.

A reet sucker

"Now Luke's on piece work, 'e's been goin' like mad. Mind thee, 'e's a shadow o' what he were. Thin as a wafer," said Job.

"Well, 'e's off today. Mun be 'avin' a rest," Benny replied.

"''s not that," advised Teddy. "'is missus rang in t'say that as she were cleanin' up, 'e disappeared."

"Disappeared, where to?" Job asked.

"Says 'er's not sure but 'er's got an idea 'e were sucked up in th''oover."

Cover-up

"Tha'd 'ave t'detonate that dust off thy face. Mun be six inches deep. 'ow long is it sin' tha's 'ad a bath?" Wally asked Claude.

"Don't like water," Claude replied. "Every month, t'missus chucks a bucket o' white-wash o' er me."

Owt to save money

"How did Zebediah get those blue marks all over him?" the Bevin Boy asked.

"It's a sort of tattooin'," Seth replied.

"Must have cost him a fortune to get them done," said the boy.

"Cost 'im nowt. 'e got em down 'ere for free," Seth advised. "An' if tha works down t'pit long enough, tha'll get some an' all."

"Great, I've always fancied a tattoo. Might as well save myself a few bob," said the Bevin Boy.

Clear and concise

"'ow much coal can tha get in thy coal-hole?" asked Bud.

"Not as much as afore," Andy replied. Used t'get a whole lot o' coal in the old coal-'ole but sin we moved we don't get as much. Mind thee, we still get quite a lot o' coal in the new coal-'ole but it's noweer near as much as in the old coal-'ole." He went on, "'ow much coal can tha get in thy coal-'ole?"

"Ain't got one an' if I 'ad, it'd take all neet t'tell thee," Bud replied.

Sprat to catch a mackerel

"Wha's up wi' Moggie? Looks down in t'dumps," Luther asked.

"Summat t'do wi' 'is missus," Isaac replied.

"Why, wha 's 'appened?"

"When 'e got 'ome las' neet, she said she really fancied a fish. So 'e went down t'chippie an' waited an 'our afore 'e got one."

"And?"

"When he got back, 'is missus 'ad run off."

"Who wi'?"

"Willie. Tha knows, one o' them Fish lads from round t'corner."

"Wha's 'e goin' t'do abaht it?"

"Wha' does think? Batter 'im, o' course."

An English lesson

The new N.C.B. flag fluttered in the breeze.

"Thowt I'd never see it," enthused Claude.

"Wha'?"

"We're pasteurised at last," came the reply.

"Aye, it's a great day. After all this time, we've been sterilised," said Wally.

"Speak for thysen," Claude answered. "Tha might 'ave been but I ain't 'avin' it done, no way."

Mirror image

"I shouldn't be here. I didn't want to come down the pit in the first place. I hate looking at that nasty, dirty, horrible coalface," said the Bevin Boy.

"Calm thysen, lad," said Seth. "Tha shouldn't keep lookin' in t'mirror."

Transfer training

"Why's that new bloke sittin' on t'pony's back an' jumpin' o'er all t'tubs?" asked Tommy.

"'eard 'e used t'be in th'ousehold Cavalry," said Henry.

Tricks of the trade

"Got t'rush. No showerin' today. I'm off t'have me palm read," shouted Robbie as the cage surfaced.

"Wha' for?" asked Cedric.

"T'see what t'future 'olds, o' course," came the reply. The next day, Robbie entered the canteen and sat with his workmates.

"'ow did it go?" queried Cedric.

"Ruddy marvellous," Robbie assured him.

"Wha' did 'er tell thee then?"

"'er said that I were a collier an' that I'd get a real wiggin' from t'wife for goin' 'ome in me muck."

"An' were 'er spot on?"

"'er give me a reet ear-bashin'."

"By gum, that's clever. Wouldn't mind 'avin' a go mysen," said Cedric.

"Tha can count us in an' all," said his workmates.

"Reet then, give us a bob each an' I'll fix it for thee for toneet," promised Robbie.

One by one, they handed over their money.

"Now, Robbie, weer does 'er live?" asked Cedric.

"Wi' me."

"Wi thee?"

"Aye, it's me missus. I won't be in so just knock on t'front door. I'll be in t'pub and thanks, lads, for t'beer money."

What a waste

"What do you call those things you put in the tub-wheels to stop them running?" asked the Bevin Boy.

"'ere we calls it a pig-tail locker," replied Erasmus.

"I believe that north of the border they call it 'scotch'" said the boy.

"'appen they do. Mind thee, they make gallons o' t'stuff up theer?"

"What?" asked the Bevin Boy.

"Whiskey."

A reet 'owler

"That's a bonny pigeon tha's got in t'loft," George said. "Bit of a fancier, art tha?"

"Aye," replied Henry.

"I thowt tha 'ad about ten of 'em," George remarked. "Weer are t'others then?"

"Cleared off last week an' didn't come back," Henry answered.

"Ne'er mind," said George. At least, tha's got one left t'keep thee goin'. Get another an' tha can start breedin' 'em again."

"Some use that is," Henry exclaimed. "It's an owl."

Emergency

"Can you smell gas?" asked the worried-looking Bevin Boy.

"Nay, tha can't smell gas down 'ere. We've checked an' it's all clear," said Midge.

"But I can still smell it," insisted the Bevin Boy.

"My mum says I've got a sensitive nose."

"All reet, tell thee what I'll do, I'll turn t'tap an' cooker off an' open all t'winders while tha goes an' gets t'Gas Board."

Master of his craft

"What does tha keep in thy snap-tin?" Cecil asked.

"Jam sandwiches," replied the Bevin Boy.

"What do you keep in yours?"

"A bit o' dry bread," came the response.

"Dry bread?" the youngster repeated.

"Aye, I usually eat mice butties. There's plenty on 'em down 'ere. Make a grand fillin'."

"The thought of it turns me off," exclaimed the Bevin Boy, turning pale.

"Don't feel hungry any more. Here, you can have my sandwiches."

"Ta," said Cecil.

As the boy disappeared down the haulage-road, Cecil turned and winked at his work-mate.

"Sithee, works every time," he said.

Born loser

"Why is Sammy looking so miserable?" asked the Bevin Boy.

"It's on account o' 'is whippet," came the reply.

"Something wrong with it?"

"Nay, nowt at a'."

"Does he race it?"

"Oh, aye."

"And does it win?"

"Never loses."

"Well, what's he got to look so glum about?"

"When Sammy races it, 'e comes last every time."

Over zealous

"Summat's got t'be done about Charlie," said Tom.

"Wha' does't mean?" asked Sam.

"Bein' an air-raid warden's gone to 'is 'ead. When 'e comes on our face, 'e keeps shoutin', 'Put that leet out'. Not turned out any coal for a week. Afore tha knows it, us'll be shuttin' up shop."

The numbers game

"'ere," said Freddie, producing a newspaper. Read it for us cos I've left me specs at 'ome."

"No good asking me," Timmy replied. "Can't read."

"Nor me," added George.

"I can," said Herbert. "Pass it 'ere. Now, lads, art ready?"

"Aye," the others agreed and settled down to listen.

"'ere we go then. It says 'ere 'twenty-one' then there's summat else an' it ends wi' 'nineteen forty-five."

"That's the ruddy date," Freddie interrupted.

"'ang on, I aren't finished yet. When I turn o' er, it says 'two' at t'top o' t'page."

"That's not proper readin'," said George.

"I'm gettin' theer though," Herbert replied. "At t'moment, I can only read numbers."

A little knowledge

"Ever been underground afore?" the Bevin Boy was asked.

"Sure have," came the reply.

"Well, tha'll be well used to it."

"Course I am."

"Weer were thee then when tha went underground?"

"In our Anderson shelter," answered the Bevin Boy.

If only

"I'm gettin' sick o' workin' underground," said Stan.

"When I come back, I'm goin' t'be summat else."

"Me, too," agreed Harry.

"Think I'll be a lord wi' a big 'ouse an' servants."

"Not me," Stan replied. "I'm comin' back as an animal."

"Wha' sort?" Harry asked.

"Dunno really," Stan scratched his head and pondered.

"Gorrit. I'm comin' back as a mole."

Your turn, Toby

Toby sat in the pit-canteen with his head in his hands. "I'll never manage. I'll never manage," he kept repeating.

"Tha's lookin' reet glum. What's up with thee?" asked Rob.

Toby looked up with tears in his eyes. "T'missus 'as left me," he sobbed.

"Cheer up, lad. Can't be all that bad. Left thee for another bloke, 'as 'er?"

"Nowt like that," Toby answered.

"Gone to t'mother-in-law's for a couple o' days an' 'er's left me a note t'do all t'shoppin', cleanin', cookin', washin' an' ironin'."

"'ard luck," said Rob. "An' you wi' ten kids an' all,"

Initiative

Over the noise of the drill, Bertie shouted, "We need a spar quick."

"Eh?" asked Solly, cupping his ear.

"A spar, quick," Bertie repeated.

"Not afore time too," said Solly.

"Been needin' one for ages down 'ere." Then he disappeared for the rest of the shift. The following day, a deputy approached Bertie.

"Don't know what's goin' on but I've got a message for thee from Solly."

"What?" asked Bertie.

"Summat about 'im comin' down in t'cage wi' a load o' beer barrels an' 'e wants know weer t'cellar is," said the deputy.

Clean air act

"Smells horrible down here," said the Bevin Boy.

"Tha's what comes o' not 'avin' any lavvies," replied Horace.

"How do you cope with it?" asked the Bevin Boy.

"Easy, just 'old thy breath like so," Horace demonstrated, pinching his nose and closing his mouth.

"And what happens if a few of the lads want to go at the same time?" the boy queried.

"Don't worry. Won't do thee any 'arm... All tha does is afore. 'old thy breath a bit longer, like this," Again he demonstrated.

"Thanks for the advice," said the Bevin Boy, looking down at the prostrate, unconscious Horace.

Misunderstanding

The miner looked at the Bevin Boy. "Come on, shape thysen. Get sprucin' up," he said.

"If you don't mind, I've spruced myself up already, thank you," Think I look quite smart in fact," came the haughty reply.

"No offence, lad," said the miner.

"I meant get them spruce props on to t'tram."

New arrival

"What's up wi' thee, Tommy?"

"Nowt. Why are tha askin'?"

"Tha's white's a sheet. Should 'ave stayed under t'blankets an' 'ad a reet good sleep."

"Been up all neet," Tommy replied. "T'missus 'as 'ad a baby."

"Congratulations, owd lad. What's tha goin' t'call it?"

"Ida."

"So her'll be called 'Ida Down' then?"

A hard fact

"Ee, that were smashin'," said Monty, awakening from a snap-time nap.

"Dreamt I were in me own pit."

"So y'are," said Willy.

"But it ain't thine."

Bowels of the earth

"It's a damned hot pit," said the Bevin Boy.

"That it is, son," Tom replied.

"Sometimes, it can get 'otter," observed their companion.

"The 'otter, the better."

"Wouldn't like to live down here," declared the Bevin Boy.

"Me neither," Tom agreed.

"But 'e does," and he pointed at their work-mate.

"Is he homeless then?" asked the Bevin Boy.

"Nay, just likes it, that's all. Made it 'is 'ome years ago."

"By the way, Tom," the boy asked.

"What's his name? I haven't seen him before."

"Nicholas," came the reply.

"But all t'lads call 'im Owd Nick."

"That explains it then," said the boy.

"Explains what?" asked Tom.

"Explains why he's got two horns on his head and a tail sticking out of his trousers."

Tempting fate

"Tha's lucky 'avin' a missus who makes 'ome-made toffee," said Hoppy.

"Gie us one o' them acid drops tha carries wi' thee." Eustace passed him the bag. Hoppy sucked away. "Aren't 'avin' one thysen?" he asked.

"Nay, never eat 'em," Eustace replied.

"Lovely," said Hoppy, as he popped another one into his mouth.

"By gum," he continued. They're real tasty. Mind thee, they don't 'alf burn thy mouth an' tongue."

"That's why I ne'er eat 'em," replied Eustace. "T'missus gets th'acid from t'chemical plant round t'corner."

Over-subscribed

The Yorkshire coalfield was well-known for its wealth of Rugby League talent.

"Eh, lad," said Billy to the Bevin Boy.

"We've got a match on this affie. We're a couple o' players short. Just shout down t'shaft an' round us up a few."

Ten minutes later, the pit had to close for the day through lack of manpower.

'Itching a lift

One day, a Bevin Boy was accompanied home by some unwelcome and uninvited guests.

"Nothing to worry about," said his father.

"In the last war, my uniform was full of 'em. He continued, "Take off your shirt, son and I'll check your body for bites."

There wasn't a mark on the boy but his father was bitten all over.

"Must be old friends looking you up, Dad," said the Bevin Boy.

In a lighter vein

The pit-men lined up outside the lamp-room.

"Here's your oil-lamp, lad," said the attendant.

"Won't be needing it today," replied the Bevin Boy.

"Why, not goln' down then?" he was asked.

"Sure am."

"Well, in that case, tha'll need a light," advised the attendant.

"Brought my own," the Bevin Boy assured him. "Yesterday, I fell over and it went out, so for a change, I've brought some candles and a box of matches."

Ambition

"Tha's been a long time down t'pit, Willie. Has't ever thowt o' retirin'?"

"You young un's are all t'same. Always askin' when I'm retirin. Expect tha's after me job then, eh?"

"Mebbe."

"Well, for thy information, I'll be packin' in after me next birthday."

"An' 'ow old will tha be then?"

"Seventy-two."

"Fancy tha'."

"Fancy wha'?"

"I were eighty las' week."

Short supply

"What does think o' this food rationin' then?"

"Not much."

"I know it's not. I'm fair starvin'."

Clear the air

"Gets thee in t'chest, don't it?"

"What's tha mean, all that dust down 'ere?"

"Nay, all that air on t'top."

The menu

It was a glorious summer's day. "Look o' er yon at all that sunshine an' we got t'go down t'pit," Bob complained.

"Nae bad for starters," Henry agreed. The shift over, they surfaced. It was pouring down.

"Look yon at all that wet an' we've only just come up t'pit," Bob moaned.

"I see wha' tha means", Henry observed. "T'starters were all reet but t'puddin's well off."

Head size

"Owd Bevin took some numbers out 'is 'at," said Harry.

"Did 'e, an' all?" asked Sandy.

"Aye, tha's why theer's so many o' these young lads down t'pit," declared Harry.

"Mun 'ave a ruddy big 'ead," Sandy said.

"Wears a big bowler 'at," Harry advised.

"That so?"

"Got to," replied Harry.

"Why so?"

"Cos 'e wouldna got enough Bevin Boys if 'e'd wore a cap," came the reply.

If the cap fits

"Reckon it's gone to 'is 'ead," said Abe.

"Talkin' ababt Paddy?" asked Charlie.

"'appen," replied Abe.

"Could be all that booze 'e knocks back," suggested Charlie.

"I'm talkin' abaht 'is new cap," Abe answered.

The merry miner

Willie returned from the bar and handed over a glass of beer to his missus.

"Glad tha's back," she said.

"Theer's a bloke o' er in t'corner who's bin watchin' thee an' me at t'same time. Don't know 'ow 'e does it. Proper weird it is."

"Nowt t'worry abaht," Willie replied.

"It's only owd Zak, 'e's cross-eyed, tha knows."

"Tha's a shame," said his missus.

"Born wi' it, were 'e?"

"Nay," Willie answered looking up at the wall-clock.

"'e comes in 'ere every day an' I reckon by now 'e'll be on 'is fifteenth pint."

26. TOMMY REMEMBERED

As I sat at my winding-engine, a dark figure approached.

"Hello, Tommy, what are you doing here?" I asked. Dimming his battery-lamp, he replied, "Thowt I'd pop by to see how tha's gettin' on. Settled in yet? Ain't easy for you youngsters down 'ere."

I thanked him for his concern and said, "Where are you off then?" to which he responded, "Got a job on just round t'bend. Oh, aye, an' if tha fancies, I'll see thee in t'canteen after t'shift."

"I'll be there, Tommy," I nodded.

I looked at him. He presented a squat, sturdy figure. Several times, I had watched him in action, working away, often alone, drawing props and ensuring that the weight of the rock above was transferred from the coalface. He was broad of shoulder and slim-waisted, with muscular arms. Wearing only shorts and clogs, his body, glistening with sweat, was streaked with dust. His work was extremely dangerous.

My companions, Barney and Steve, were driving a face and for the next hour or so, I continued to draw and lower their tubs.

A light appeared behind me and I saw that it was Fred. He was doing his best to run up the gradient.

"Quick," he gasped, "There's been one helluva fall and Tommy's under it. We're really going to need some help. Think he might be dead. Get Barney and Steve. Can't get him out on my own."

The three of us followed Fred to where Tommy lay. All we could see was a pair of ankles, protruding from under a massive slab which covered most of his body, including his face. We noticed a deep cone-shaped hole in the roof.

"That's weer it's come from," observed Barney.

"We'll never get him out," said Fred, the newly-arrived Bevin Boy.

"Mun talk like that, son," admonished Steve. 'We'll do it."

"'Ang on, Tommy, lad, we'll 'ave thee out in a jiff," Barney tried to reassure him. Painfully slowly and after what seemed an age, we managed to remove the rock from his body. He was in a dreadful state. His legs and face were cut and bleeding and skin was torn from his chest, at every move, he groaned in agony. We rendered what little first-aid we could and gently lowered him on to the stretcher, which Fred had produced. I saw that Tommy was now shaking uncontrollably. I tore off my thick sweat-shirt and placed it on him.

"Speed's the thing," said Barney. "Can thee manage? I'll keep watch in case theer's any more falls."

We lifted the stretcher and painstakingly negotiated the tunnels and various air-doors. It was a delicate and arduous task. We experienced the early stages of heat exhaustion but, at last, we saw the welcoming lights of the pit-bottom. My shirt was handed back to me and a blanket was tenderly placed over Tommy. It was pointless trying to offer him words of encouragement for he had lapsed into an unconscious state. We watched the start of his slow ascent in the cage and reluctantly returned to our duties.

"Think he'll make it?" I asked Steve.

"Canna tell. 'e's in pretty bad shape," came his response.

For the rest of the shift, the mood of our little group was sombre and hardly a word was spoken. We were lost in our own thoughts.

We were relieved to return to the surface and breathe in the cool, bracing air. I did not see Tommy in the canteen that night, or any other night for that matter.

It was confirmed that his pelvis had been smashed and that there were rib fractures. He spent many months in hospital and, thanks to the skill of the medical team who tended him and his own indomitable spirit, he survived. He never went underground again.

Mining communities are all too aware of the daily dangers that beset their menfolk but there are many who are completely unaware of the dramas that are enacted under their feet, day by day.

A MOTHER'S FORGIVENESS

Black diamonds nourish a nation at war,
Life-blood of our land and we gaze in awe
At that glistening face, compressed through years.
Yet Mother Earth's anger can hasten our fears.

We are her minions. She wears the crown,
Enduringly patient, casting occasional frown
On those who toil far down below:
For true it is, we reap as we sow.

Wounded, she groans as men pick their plunder.
Her vengeance is wreaked when rock splits asunder.
Myriad shards fall, scatter and spread
As our Mother's wrath brings added dread.

But forgiveness lies there, in the green grass above,
For all living things are born of her love.
Since time began, she has withstood the test
And will gently embrace us in final rest.

D. Hollows

27. DON'T BLAME THE WATER

After a hard shift, we thoroughly enjoyed ourselves in the showers. The sound of men, some singing, some whistling, swilling off the dust and grime from their tired bodies, echoed through the building.

Finished at last, I stepped out of the cubicle and entered the locker-room to dry myself off.

A small group of men stood in a circle and I listened to their hearty laughter. In the midst of them and protecting his modesty, was Henry.

"Gerroff," he shouted as a couple of the lads flicked him with their towels.

"By gum, lad, that's a bonny wash tha's had," said one. "If I was thee, son, I'd get mysen off to t'doctor quick. Looks like tha's got t'plague or summat," observed another.

"What doest mean, plague?" asked Henry, looking very worried.

Came the reply, 'Well, look at thee. Tha's got streaks all o' er thee."

I observed that there were dark streaks on his face and shoulders running down to his waist.

"I told thee afore, I can't get clean. T'water mun be dirty or maybe t'pipes are all blocked up," Henry said.

I stared at his broad, muscular back. The nodules of his spine were red and raw, obviously where he had frequently caught himself against protruding timber shoring. On his left shoulder, forehead and face, he carried the marks of the miner - blue scars caused by coaldust settling into open wounds that heal over, a form of tattooing, in fact.

"Tell thee what," said Al, "Go back in t'showers and have another go. Mebbe it's just thine that's pouring mucky water. Try another one. You can't go wom to t'missus with them marks all o'er thee."

Henry obeyed and returned to the shower-room. Several minutes later, he returned.

"Nay," he affirmed. "I've tried a different shower and t'water's just t'same." Again, he was covered in black streaks. At this, we all burst into loud laughter.

"What's up?" asked Henry.

Al replied, "What's up, Henry? I'll tell thee what's up. It might help if tha takes off thy helmet afore tha goes into t'showers.

True enough, the helmet was adorned by a big blob of grease to which a thick layer of coaldust had adhered.

I am pleased to report that Henry returned home looking spick and span.

DUST AND GRIME

The dust and grime rule everywhere.
Feet, hands, faces, in our hair:
But its days are numbered by a mightier power
For our foe surrenders to the pit-head shower.

Comfort and cleansing by water and soap,
Carbolic, not scented and a new-born hope
We'll emerge baby-pink, just a fleeting lift
Until the next morn when we start a new shift.

The dust and grime play a waiting game,
Silent and subtle, no feelings of shame.
Then the conflict resumes yet once more,
A daily ritual, an endless chore.

Carbolic, not scented and a new-born hope.
Long may our trust lie in water and soap.
Smiles all around, not even a frown
Until today when those showers broke down.

D. Hollows

28. A BRUSH WITH THE PAST

My education had taught me that when one ventures deep underground, one mustn't be surprised to find oneself surrounded by a primeval world.

That night, I lay on my back and my eyes focused on a huge grey slab of rock above my head. There they were, an abundance of fossils, a palaeontologist's dream. An assortment of seashells, including scallops, lay like a huge canopy. Their markings were perfect and so clear. Nearby, I observed part of a tree-trunk, oval in shape and some three inches across. I recall that it reminded me of a human wrist. I tried to trace its direction but it disappeared, embedded between the coal and the rock. At intervals, there were off-shoots and branches, bearing a myriad of tiny leaves showing their veins. I marvelled at the thought that this once mighty forest giant, now compressed and looking dignified in its silence, had lain there for so long. There were countless ferns which formed pretty patterns round the tree and I was reminded of a king and his courtiers, frozen in time, I found it stimulating to be among a world formed over three hundred million years ago.

One fossil, in particular, attracted my attention. It was about seven inches long with what appeared to be, a head and a tail. It lay there in a rectilinear pose and looked serpentine. With my companion's permission, I borrowed his pick and gently prised it out. Its body bore markings and on closer examination, I saw that there was a mouth and two protrusions on the head which looked very much like eyes.

"See thee, looks just like a snake," Barney confirmed, peering over my shoulder. "What's tha goin' t'do wi' it?"

"When I get home, I'll take it the museum," I replied. "Maybe, the curator will be able to identify it."

"Good idea," Barney agreed.

The curator handled it carefully and commented, "It is most certainly snake-like, possibly the fossilised remains of a big serpent. Leave it with me and I will try to identify it."

At the time, so much was happening. It wasn't long before V.E. Day and later, V.J. Day were being celebrated, marked by both extreme joy and deep sorrow. Caught up in this unreal and unfamiliar atmosphere, I forgot about the fossil. That is, until recently, when I spoke to an official at the museum. He was very interested in my story which began some sixty years ago and promised to search all available donor cards. He added that many wartime records no longer existed and stated that for storage purposes, numerous exhibits had been transferred to the basement which later became flooded. The resultant damage led to the discarding of many items. It transpired that there wasn't any reference to my find. Naturally, I was disappointed.

My desire to confirm my belief that I had handled a reptile from a past age prompted me to seek out an expert from the University of Manchester. I supplied him with the facts and was delighted to learn that in all probability, I had found a fossilised snake.

Sadly, the proof has gone forever but I can console myself in the knowledge that, serpent or no serpent, I had been privileged to touch the face of pre-history.

ODE TO WONDROUS NATURE

Above me lie fossils, row upon row:
Trees, leaves and scallops caught in the glow.
Time becomes one in that lonely place.
They look so serene, so full of grace.

"Disturb us not," I hear them say,
"But gaze in wonder and awe, we pray.
Long have we lain in Mother Earth
And came soon after her galactic birth.

Tales we could tell of days gone by,
When we, too, could see the azure sky.
Once, like you, we moved and breathed,
Led by whatever life decreed.

May the Lord now grant us peaceful sleep,
In earth's darkness, warm and deep.
There are things unseen that still remain,
For man to learn and man to gain.

This day, you have seen a little, my son
And we promise you there is yet more to come.
Now we must rest for future years.
Goodbye, young friend and hush, no tears."

D. Hollows

29. EAVESDROPPERS

The shift over, I showered and joined my friend, Arnold, who had preceded me into the canteen, He had selected a table near to the counter.

"I've got you a cuppa," he said, for which I thanked him. Then, he leaned toward me and whispered, "You can't miss this. Listen to those two prattling on." He pointed at Kitty and Tess, two of our canteen ladies who were engaged in deep but loud, conversation.

"What's going on?" I asked.

"Sh, sh," Arnold tapped his nose. "Just bend your ears. Makes your mind boggle." Obviously, he had heard something that I had missed.

"I'm sick of him," said Kitty. "Absolutely fed up. I keep telling him, I'll walk out on him one day."

"Don't upset yourself," advised Tess. "Men aren't worth it. Glad I'm not wed."

At this, Kitty began to sob and blubber. Tess put a comforting arm around her shoulder. "Here, love, you can borrow my hankie."

Kitty accepted the offer, wiped her eyes, blew hard and handed it back. "Keep it or better still give it me back when you've washed it," said Tess.

"It's all that woman's fault," Kitty went on. "I blame her for everything. He's always down at her house."

Arnold smiled. "Hey up," he said. "Sounds as though her husband's having an affair. I wouldn't like to be in his clogs. Kitty's a big, strapping woman."

The conversation continued.

"She's always tempting him away from home. It's been going on since the day I met him twenty years go," complained Kitty.

"Not so good for the kids," observed Tess.

"We haven't got any," came the reply. "When he's not with her, he's in the bookies."

"I meant, if you had kids," Tess responded. "Look, why don't you go to her house and have it out with her once and for all?"

"What's the use? "came the wailing cry. "It won't stop him, no matter what I say. The only time he doesn't go is when it's wet."

"He only goes there on dry days?" asked Tess. "What do you think they're up to?" Arnold winked at me.

"Nothing like that," Kitty answered. "He can't tidy her garden when it's raining."

"Is that all? What the devil are you so worried about?" Tess queried.

Kitty ignored the comment and went on, "I'm just fed up with her. He needn't come crying to me. I want nothing to do with it."

"Do you know this woman?" Tess questioned.

"Course I do. It's my old man's sister. She's working him too hard and it's bound to happen again. When it does, he'll get no sympathy from me."

"When what happens?" Tess asked.

"When he gets another hernia," Kitty replied. "He'll have to wear a truss again and he hates trusses."

THE PIT-HEAD CANTEEN

Nothing equals the gossip in the pit-head canteen.
Current affairs, the future and what might have been.
More fun than the wireless or printed news,
Exchanging ideas and the expounding of views.

Willie, the collier, complains of his twinges,
While Henry advises oily salves for his hinges.
Willie's a fine chap, I hasten to say,
For it's pints all round when he gets his pay.

Doreen, the quiet one, butters the bread.
As long as I've known her, not a word has she said.
It is claimed that still waters can run very deep.
Her hypnotic buttering oft sends one to sleep.

There's chitter and chatter, the clatter of plates,
Whispers and laughter as couples make dates.
Silvery tea-urns, hissing out steam.
It's a pleasure to sit here, if only to dream.

News of the departed and babes newly-born
And the latest update on Florrie's corn.
Old Benny coughs, then a sneeze and a wheeze.
Sheer stimulation among folk such as these.

Amy's cigarette has a full inch of ash
Which falls and disappears in a panful of mash.
"Look, lads," she says. "Here's a dish you should savour.
Made it myself and it's got a great flavour.

Right, boys, come and get it," she smilingly cries
But we've spotted the deed and go for the pies.
From Ben,"Amy, I grant that tha's good at thy craft
Eat mash an' ash? Nay. Tha mun think we're daft."

A group of young Bevin Boys, so fresh of face,
Add to the colour of this busy place.
Dialect phrases, their task for the day,
Gaining success and acceptance in every way.

Alfred, now wiser, tells over the din,
Of the time he mislaid his trusty snap-tin.
What followed next was not very nice,
For his beloved jam-butties were devoured by mice.

Pale faces leave, black faces arrive,
Like the buzz and the hum of a human hive.
Courage lies here and sacrifice too
And victory's spirit in glorious hue.

I hear one mutter, "Ta, love." Another says, "Please."
And Barney, the joker quips, "Any more cheese?"
From Edna, a grimace. Then comes the reply,
"Don't tha yet know it's in short supply?"

Jim, from the lamp-room, has a plastered thumb.
He affirms that it's healing but still feeling numb.
With an armful of washing, he got caught in a tangle.
When helping his wife, he fell straight in the mangle.

Dave sits alone, licking his lips.
He's just finished off a plateful of chips.
Striking a match, he lights up his pipe,
At peace with the world, a contented type.

Though near to the shafts, it seems rather droll,
We can discard all thoughts of the dreaded hole,
For here, comrades forget, relax and feel free
As they drown their fatigue with copious tea.

Rays of sunlight bathe the room
And soon, some will enter that world of gloom.
Cups are emptied, farewells are said.
If it's not on the shift, it's off home to bed.

There's a war to be fought and coal to be won.
Much hardship ahead ere our job is done.
United we stand in a common cause
Those wheels must keep turning with barely a pause.

When conflict is ended and peace is declared,
We will remember those days which we proudly shared,
Below ground, above ground, in the pit-head canteen,
The Bevin Boys too, were part of that scene.

As the hours pass by and shadows fall,
Much older now, our lads still recall
The challenge, the toil, the sweat and the tears
That beset us all in our early years.

The miners, our mentors, became our close friends:
An enduring bond that never ends
And honoured forever. We were so young then
When we served King and country with those giants of men.

D. Hollows

30. A LUCKY ESCAPE

The only trouble with a regular oil-lamp was that, in a split second, one could be enveloped in total darkness. A slight stumble, a sudden jerk, could flood the wick to such an extent that it would extinguish itself. Without companions nearby or a battery-lamp as back-up, one could be cast into inky blackness.

Such was the case with Benny. He had been working alone in an isolated area when he slipped and his lamp went out.

It later transpired that he had sat in the same spot for some time before deciding to seek out his workmates. He knew that his cries would go unheard for they were too far away. Gingerly, he rose to his feet, felt the tunnel wall and began to edge his way forward, inch by inch.

Having completed their shift, the miners surfaced. It was noted that Benny's tally-disc had not been claimed. "Maybe he's doing a spot of overtime," it was suggested.

The hours passed. The next shift came and went. Benny's disc remained unclaimed.

Then there was real concern. A rescue party was organised. Hour after hour, they searched but all to no avail. They began to fear the worst.

An underground meeting was hastily arranged, to pool information and to devise a strategy. "Could he be buried under a fall?" they wondered. Nearer the mark, one proposed that he had most probably experienced a problem with his lamp. It couldn't be re-ignited. They knew that without his lamp, he could be anywhere. Time was of the essence. They searched various districts but still there was no indication of his whereabouts. The rescue party was relieved by another, which didn't meet with any success. Benny had completely vanished.

On the third day, it was decided to extend the search.

It was felt that perhaps the old workings would reveal some clues.

The steep, uphill climb taxed the searchers' strength to the limit.

They followed the route of a long-disused tramway, catching their backs on broken and projecting timbers and still detecting the lingering smell of charred wood, a legacy of the 1930 explosion.

"No one here," observed one. "Shaft's just ahead."

Disappointed, they decided to go back and began to walk down the gradient.

Suddenly, there was a shout. As one of the group turned, his lamp picked out a motionless figure, lying face down with one arm outstretched.

"Found him," he cried. Benny was still barely conscious. He was absolutely exhausted and completely dehydrated.

As one of the rescuers put it, "He's a very lucky lad. Another two yards and he'd have been down the shaft."

31. "TOM" FOOLERY

Old Tom worked on the regular night-shift. Well, perhaps that is an over-statement. True, he went down with us and at one stage, was given the responsibility of supervising our small group of three Bevin Boys. Indeed, there was little evidence of Tom's workmanship. He liked to sleep. Most nights, he would sit on a little wooden box in a manhole and doze off for an hour or two. We undertook the tasks that he set us and the fact that he was snoozing did not bother us unduly. At least, he wasn't continually peering over our shoulders and after all, he was in his sixties and we felt that after a lifetime in the industry, he merited a bit of relaxation.

Although we worked in a very hot mine, Tom always wore a thick jacket and a muffler. In his waist-coat pocket and held by a pendulous chain, he carried an enormous silver time-piece which rang out the hours.

He was a short, stocky man. He hadn't any immediate relatives and he had lived in a nearby lodging-house for many years. He had iron-grey hair and sported a matching Kaiser Bill moustache. He wouldn't have looked out of place wearing a spiked helmet.

When Scouse, one of our trio, first set eyes on him, he exclaimed, "Gerra a load o' that, whack, he looks like a German. Hope he's on our side."

"Old Tom's a local lad and as Lancashire as clogs and hot-pot," Colin assured him.

One night during snap-time, the three of us sat outside what we termed 'Old Tom's Grotto', munching away at our sandwiches.

"Listen to that snoring, lads. Sounds worse than the Mersey Ferry," quipped Scouse and added "Tell you what, we could have a bit of fun here."

"What do you mean'?" I asked.

"Well," he responded, "I've got a length of thread in my pocket. If we tie a bit of paper to the end of it, we could dangle it over his mouth to see how far he can blow it."

Taking it in turns, we followed Scouse's instructions, but now Tom's snoring was so regular that the paper maintained a steady, even swing and it was obvious that there could never be a winner

"Tell you what," said Scouse, "Might be more interesting if we try something else." From his pocket, he withdrew another piece of thread which he snapped and shared out.

"Now this is serious stuff. This is a bet and the loser buys breakfast in the canteen. What you have to do is tie the thread to the end of his moustache without waking him up."

Colin and I looked aghast at each other but a free breakfast in the canteen wasn't to be sniffed at.

In his deft way, Scouse succeeded first time. Old Tom slept on. I, too, got away with it. Came Colin's turn. "Good, lad," whispered Scouse, "You're getting there." Tom stirred, stretched out his right arm which brushed Colin's shoulder and which in turn, threw him completely off balance. Still holding the thread, he lost his footing and fell with such force that I fully expected to see Tom minus his moustache. Miraculously, it remained intact.

With a start, Tom awoke.

"What the 'ell's goin' on?" he bawled.

"Nothing, Tom," we answered in unison.

"Well, who the 'ell's been tying thread to me 'tache then?" The evidence was there for all to see. He glared down at Colin and shouted, "On tha' feet, lad. There'll be no nappin' on my shift an' that goes for you two an' all. Now get on with that stone-dustin.'" Promptly, we obeyed and worked as if pursued by demons.

"Suppose we did Tom a good turn really," said Scouse. Sleeping underground isn't allowed." Our tasks completed, we returned down the haulage-road to report to Tom. Of him, there was no sign.

"Wonder if he's all right?" murmured Colin.

"Course he is. Look," Scouse pointed.

On a box in a man-hole sat Tom, fast asleep and snoring more loudly than ever. Incidentally, the bet was declared null and void.

32. SALT OF THE EARTH

I felt very privileged when I was transferred to the H2 coalface and became 'sprog-man' to a coal-cutting team. We were several thousand feet deep and quite a long way from the pit-bottom. Ours was an upcast shaft and on that face which was only several feet high, the heat sapped our energy so quickly. The water, which ran under us, was always warm.

My job was to pick out holes in the roof and floor (our lads used the terms, Kench and Warrant), place the steel noose attached to the cutter into a sturdy metal bar and insert the bar at an angle into the holes. The machine-operator would turn on the power, tighten the wire and the cutter would move toward me, crab-like and tearing at the base of the seam. The whirring picks were deafening and the air was black with choking dust.

After an hour or so, we needed replacement picks and I was instructed to go to the pit-bottom to collect them. This I did and returned some fifty minutes later. It was a relief to get off that face and to feel the draughts from the two air-doors on my fairly long and arduous journey. Several times I caught my spine on broken protruding timbers, but felt that a visit to the showers at the end of the shift would help minimise the burning sensation.

Repairs were effected and the work began in earnest. The cutter-men were on one side of the machine and I, alone, on the other.

Suddenly and without any warning, there was a very loud cracking noise and down came part of the roof. I had witnessed roof-falls before but until that moment,

Colliers underground (Mr. Simm).

97

I had never been personally involved. Instantly, the power was cut and for several minutes, there was an eerie silence. Then came a loud shout, "Fall, fall." I was in an unbearably cramped space with rock before me and behind me. The dust around me was choking and so thick that my battery-lamp could not penetrate it. I felt that my eyesight was fading fast and to reassure myself, I held a finger close to my face but could not see it. Coughing and spluttering, I awaited the next fall for the ground around and above me was grumbling angrily. Fortunately, it did not materialise.

It was a strange experience. I felt that I was a spectator rather than a participant. The whole incident seemed unreal. I cannot explain it but in that restricted space, I could feel the presence of others, unseen, unheard but caring and I felt swamped by an over-whelming love. I felt resigned to the inevitable and experienced a wonderful sensation of great peace. "So be it", I thought. I must have remained in this state of euphoria for some time.

The silence was broken by a loud shout, which intruded into my reverie. "Derek, is tha all reet, lad?" to which I replied, "Yes, thanks, I think I'm in one piece."

"We'll get thee out, son," another cried... and they did.

These men had lived and worked in similar situations, day in and day out, year after year. They had the courage to rescue me knowing full well what might happen to them.

Little wonder that I regard them as the salt of the earth.

GRATITUDE

Roaring and crab-like, the machine moves on,
Grinding, biting and spewing coal.
The first cut has all but gone
And our trust lies in the Lord.

Clattering pans and belts that run
Carry our plunder to final light.
So much to do ere work is done
And our trust lies in the Lord.

Splintered timbers, a warning shout:
Our rocky blanket groans and falls.
In haste, men crawl to make it out
And our trust lies in the Lord.

But one remains in a choking tomb,
In darkness, complete and sealed.
Is this, for him, his time of doom?
And his trust lies in the Lord.

All around, in that silent place,
Comes enshrouding warmth and love,
Sensing the nearness of a Divine Grace
And his trust lies in the Lord.

A cry beyond, a helping hand,
Then frees him from his grave,
Saved by the valour of a brotherly band
And for that, I give thanks to my Lord.

D. Hollows

One can appreciate that being trapped on a low coalface must be a traumatic experience. For some weeks after the incident, my sleep was fitful and the light in my bedroom was never dimmed.

I have referred to my awareness of silent forces in that confined space and doubtless, there will be those who will propose a seemingly logical explanation. Perhaps it was a chemical brain reaction to a situation inducing uncertainty, shock and ensuing panic. However, as protagonist, I know what I experienced at the time and the peace and warmth that I felt was akin to the love of a mother for her newly-born.

The initial chill of fear has now all but dissipated and the episode is enshrouded by the overwhelming comfort that I received from sources unknown.

During the years that have followed, I have witnessed and been privy to several incidents where there has been an awareness of an indeterminate force, unseen and unheard and have met so many who have had similar sensations. With so much supportive evidence, one is bound to conclude that there must be something as yet undiscovered. This reinforces my firm belief that in God's great universe, there remain mysteries which lie unresolved and awaiting interpretation.

33. IMPROVISE

Discussing toilets is usually a delicate matter and not always to everyone's taste.

So it was one day in 1944 when a young Bevin boy entered our district. He was a tall, slim youth. His helmet was placed at a jaunty angle and unlike the rest of us, he wore that appeared to be a brand-new Harris Tweed jacket. We were amazed and amused to note that he also wore a pair of expensive-looking yellow gloves. He looked more like a country squire than an under-ground worker.

"Morning," he said. "How are you today?" He spoke with a refined accent.

"All reet, ta," Tommy replied and went on, "What's tha wearin' them gloves for? Won't last long down 'ere, I can tell thee."

"I intend to be a surgeon when I'm released," came the answer. "Can't have my hands ruined, y'know. Incidentally, my name's Clive and you are?" He looked at the three of us, took off his right glove and extended his hand which we shook warmly and introduced ourselves.

"Damn it," he remarked, looking at his bare, blackened hand. "I'm getting filthy already" and he replaced his glove.

"The purpose of my visit," he said to Barney, "Is to find the toilets."

"Didn't tha go when tha were on t'top?" asked Tommy.

"Afraid not," came the reply. "Thought I could last out but I've been taken rather short."

"Well," Barney pointed, "If tha follows this road, then turns reet at t'bottom and carries straight on, tha'll find t'toilets."

"Not an old tub with a lid on, I presume?" Clive queried.

"Nay, no chance," Barney assured him. "They're proper lavs wi' wash-bowls and a bloke who looks after 'em."

"Thank you, my good man," Clive exclaimed. "Must rush. See you again" and he disappeared. down the haulage-road.

Some time later, he returned. "Sure you've given me the right directions?" he asked Barney. "I can't find them anywhere."

Tommy interrupted, "Barney told thee to carry straight on, lad. He meant to t'pit bottom an' up t'shaft to t'surface. They're up theer."

"Thanks a lot," said Clive, with noted sarcasm and continued, "But look here, chaps, you must appreciate my dilemma. I can't hold out much longer. What can I do?"

Barney looked long and hard at him. "Tha's got two choices," he advised. "If tha does it down 'ere, tha won't be popular cos we'll all suffer, so t'best thing t'do is use tha gloves."

Sequel. We never discovered if Clive accepted Barney's suggestion but thereafter, he was seen minus his gloves and with hands that matched ours.

34. ALL MOD CONS

As we dried off in the pit-head baths, Tommy looked long and hard at me. "Wha's up, son? Tha doesn't seem thysen today," he remarked.

"Just wha' I were thinkin' an' all," added Henry.

"Feeling a bit rough. Queasy stomach," I replied, at which Tommy asked me to list my symptoms. "Reet then, stick out thy tongue," he ordered.

"An' don't forget t'check 'is eyeballs," suggested Albert.

"Look, Tommy, 'is eyes 'as got black in 'em," Henry pointed excitedly, as if he had made a great discovery.

"Stop puttin' t'wind up 'im," admonished Tommy. "I'm t'First Aider 'ere. That there black's nowt but coaldust" and he assumed the authority of one who was fully conversant with his medical manual. Prognosis followed diagnosis.

"I reckon tha's got a dose o' Bevin Boys' lurgie," he pronounced.

"What's that?" I asked.

"Well, it's wha' tha picks up down t'pit," advised Henry. "Us owd timers is used to it. Last time it got me were twenty year ago. Ne'er touched me sin'."

"Nor me," said Tommy.

"Me neither," Albert agreed.

"What causes it?" I questioned.

"Comes o'not 'avin proper lavvies down theer," Tommy answered. "You Bevin lads are bound t'get it sooner or later. Tha'll feel bad, o'course but it won't kill thee. Now get straight off wom an' take to thy bed."

So it was that after a painful and uncomfortable journey, I arrived home.

"Expect you are hungry, son," said my mother. "I'll fry some bacon and egg for your tea."

The mere thought of consuming food was nauseating. I murmured my thanks and dragged myself into bed.

The doctor confirmed that I was suffering from gastro-enteritis and I was given the necessary medication. My father who had been a medic during the Gallipoli campaign, prescribed a light diet which in spite of our meagre rations, was lovingly prepared by my mother. As the days passed, I regained my strength and vigour. Two weeks later, I was pronounced fit enough to resume my underground duties.

I entered the changing-room. Of my work-mates, there was no sign.

"Where are they?" I asked Billy from the lamp-room.

"Who does't mean?" he queried.

"Tommy, Henry and Albert," I replied.

"Oh, them. They've got t'lurgie, lad. Took bad same time as thee. Course, tha knows 'ow tha gets it. Comes o' not 'avin'...."

"Toilets down the pit," I finished.

"Aye, that's reet. Mebbe one day, they'll 'ave t'sense t'put some flush lavvies down theer," Billy suggested.

"No chance," interrupted Sam, the collier.

"Why not?" I questioned.

"Simple, son," Sam answered. "Cos down theer we'll be nigh on three thousand feet under t'sewers."

For the record, one year later, I suffered a repeat performance of the same malady.

35. A CHANCE CONVERSATION

During a snap-time conversation, one of my mining companions who had a keen interest in transport systems, referred to a local canal.

"The Sankey and St. Helens Canal was cut in the 1750's. It was used to carry goods to Liverpool," he informed me and then went on to tell me about a long-past annual ceremony. "We all went in our Sunday best like everyone else," he said. Obviously, it had been an eagerly anticipated day by the local inhabitants.

"What took place?" I asked.

"Well, it was all to do with the railway and wagon-works," he replied and continued, "Anyone who was anybody would stand outside the door of Stephenson's Cottage and we watched as another link was added to the Railway queen's chain of office. It reminded everyone of the importance of the industry to the area, a sort of commemoration, in fact."

I recalled that conversation some twenty years later when my parents purchased the cottage. It lay at the foot of Emmett's Brow in Earlestown, Lancashire.

From the door which had once been the scene of an interesting ritual, one could look across the spacious front gardens containing a variety of shrubs and an abundance of roses at the mighty viaduct, known an the Nine Arches which traversed the Sankey Canal. Each span measured fifty feet and the project was completed at a cost of £45,000.

I spent many happy hours in Stephenson's cottage. From the front windows of the low-beamed living-room it was not difficult to visualise that great man watching the surveyors, engineers and builders at work some several hundred yards away.

Stephensons Cottage.

Attached to the premises was his work-shop, containing a bench at which, I believe, he spent many hours poring over his plans. There were accompanying obstacles and especially so over Chat Moss, a swampy area. To counteract this, large bales of cotton were sunk deep to absorb the moisture and to ensure firmer foundations.

When finally completed, the tracks echoed to the sound of coal-laden wagons from Haydock and surrounding areas. There was a demand for fuel for this was the Industrial Revolution.

Often, as I stood in the garden I felt transported back to another age, to become a part of that great era.

It saddens me to think that the building no longer exists. All that remain are a retaining wall at the rear of the cottage and of course, my own nostalgic memories of days gone by.

36. BRIAN CLOUGH, A MAN OF STATURE

The late Brian Clough, successively the Manager of Derby County and Nottingham Forest Football Clubs, developed an excellent rapport with the local miners and was highly regarded by them.

This interaction was bound to leave its mark and as with so many who toiled in the mine, he was acclaimed for his forthright manner and straight-faced good humour.

The story goes that on one occasion, he took members of his team underground and declared, "Now, gentlemen, I have brought you down here to show you what really hard work is all about." He recognised the demands made on those who were obliged to win the coal, often against over-whelming odds. Without doubt, his players could not fail to emerge from the darkness much wiser and with renewed determination to succeed.

In most cases, nick-names bestow great respect on the recipient and it is little wonder that he was affectionately referred to as "Cloughie."

During the 1984–85 miners' strike, he visited some of those who were involved and arranged free admittance to matches for men who were experiencing financial hardship.

This generous act symbolises the true spirit of the miner-loyalty, dedication, compassion and contribution. These characteristics have always been of paramount importance among all mining communities. Although not a miner himself, Brian Clough exemplified the qualities of all those whose roots are embedded in the industry.

In the 1970's one of our pupils was signed to play for Derby County. On a home-visit, he spoke to me of his career and was full of praise for his Manager. "All of us have the utmost respect for Cloughie," he assured me and went on, "He gets straight to the point and won't stand for any nonsense. He is a father-figure to the whole team, positive, caring and a very fine man." With those words, there can be no greater tribute.

37. A BEVIN BOY'S NIGHT OUT

The shift over, I showered and returned home. The rest of the day was mine and after deliberation, I decided to go for a stroll. I had not travelled far when I had a very pleasant surprise. Approaching me from the opposite direction was my old chum.

"Eric," I exclaimed. "What are you doing here? It's great to see you again." We shook hands.

"Likewise," he smiled. "I'm on my way to see you. I've got a spot of leave."

From early childhood, we had been close friends and some five years previously we had waited together outside our local barracks to witness the return of a group of walking-wounded soldiers who had been rescued from the Dunkirk beaches. I recalled that Eric had vowed to join the Camerons after seeing a Highlander pipe the dejected men from their transports. Now here he was, his dream realised and a private in the 51st Highland Division (Camerons). He was over six feet tall, broad of shoulder and dark-haired with a complexion which though normally rosy, was now deeply-tanned and in sharp contrast to the pallor I had acquired underground. In fact, he was the picture of clean living and complete fitness. In his uniform, he was magnificent with beribboned and bobbed glengarry, battle-dress top, kilt and socks, one of which partially concealed a dirk.

We relaxed in the sitting-room (often referred to in Lancashire as the 'parlour') and over cups of tea and large slices of my mother's home-made cake, engaged in lengthy conversation.

"How's Germany and where are you now based?" I asked.

"I'm in Berlin. We've passed through some really devastated towns, I must say. But you know, in Berlin the lights are on and there's stuff in the shop-windows that we haven't seen here since before the war." He continued, "By the way, how's the job going?"

"Not too badly," I replied. "We are still getting the coal out and I consider it an honour to work with such fine men."

"In my book, they're ruddy heroes. They must be to work down there. You wouldn't catch me doing it. No way," observed Eric. Eventually our discourse ended when he added, "Tell you what. How about going to the flicks tonight?"

"You're on," I affirmed and early that evening, we made our way into Warrington Town Centre.

"Fancy a bite to eat?" Eric asked. I nodded my assent and we went to the Red Rose Milk Bar in Friars' Gate where we ate, drank and watched the clientèle. It was a busy place. There were groups of airmen, a gathering of pensioners, parents with children, couples some holding hands and oblivious to those around and several G.I.'s from the nearby Burtonwood U.S. Air Force Base. Our attention was then drawn to two young men who sat in a corner and were deep in conversation. Each had a suitcase and from time to time, they approached the tables and offered items for sale to the patrons.

"Seedy-looking pair," I whispered. "Spivs," Eric replied. I've seen more than enough of their ilk. While we're serving Crown and country for a pittance, they're cashing in selling Black Market goods." We observed them as they went from table to table but it was obvious that their efforts went unrewarded. Our meal over, we joined the queue outside the Odeon Cinema in Buttermarket Street and eventually gained admittance. At the conclusion of the programme, we stood for the National Anthem and left. Nearby, was another cinema, the Empire and as we passed the main entrance, the audience began to spill out. Casually and chatting away, we negotiated the throng and walked toward our bus stop. Suddenly and unexpectedly, we were joined by the two men whom we instantly recognised as the wide-boys in the milk-bar. "Hey, love, gerra load o' that," said one addressing Eric. "You're a right stunner in that skirt. How about a drink in the Red Lion? His companion joined in with," Yeah, duck, we'll show you a good time." The jibes continued and I could see that Eric was becoming increasingly embarrassed by their incessant goading and especially so as passers-by, on hearing their comments, turned and stared hard at us. Eric was an extremely tolerant soul but he wasn't to be meddled with. "Hold on, Dek, I'm getting a bit fed up with this," he muttered between clenched teeth. We stopped. The two behind us stopped. Slowly, Eric adjusted his glengarry and his battle-dress. As he bent down to straighten one of his socks, his hand deliberately brushed against the hilt of his dirk. Knowing him, there was no question of his even considering using it. At least, not in those circumstances. I turned and glared at our uninvited guests. The one with the loud voice looked down at Eric's sock, nudged his companion and whispered a few words. In an instant, they ran past us, dropping their cases and spilling the contents as they did so. They shot round Burton's corner and disappeared from view. I believe that a new Olympic record was set that night. From the onlookers, there was laughter and applause for Eric's response which had put two seedy characters to flight. All in all, it had been an enjoyable and eventful evening. It is said that a picture can summon up a thousand words. That night, Eric's simple gesture spoke volumes.

38. CONSOLATION

Thankfully, the war was over at last. In retrospect, my contribution as a Bevin Boy seems to have been minimal but perhaps I made my mark when I won a competition open to all mineworkers in the United Kingdom.

A slogan was required to mark the impending nationalisation of the industry which took place in January, 1947. My submission, 'Out of darkness, light' was accepted. Adopted by Somerset, Herald of Arms, it was translated into the Latin 'E Tenebris Lux'.

In that dust-laden gloom and among a rare breed of men, I learned what comradeship' courage and sacrifice really mean.

Thanks to them and to other members of the mining community, I entered that darkness as a boy and finally emerged into the light of manhood.

The lights go on again.

A RAY OF HOPE

In darkest caverns, my thoughts will stray to better things,
To meadows, luscious green and wet with dew,
Thorny hedgerows, the scents of Spring and hark, a bird sings,
Echoing the chorus of the early year.

Above me, people pass and speak but I hear them not,
For they are distant and think not of me,
Confined below where waters run and air is hot:
But I am with my brothers and not alone.

Black diamonds glisten and fall in rays of shafted light,
As our nation's blood pours forth:
Shaking pans and whirring belts sustain survival's fight
And my thoughts turn again to scents of Spring.

Comes the rumble, like a giant aroused, trickling and trailing dust.
Falling rock and pitiful moans.
A brother entombed, lies still and gone: the cost of coal unjust
And a world removed from the scents of Spring.

The day will dawn when men will say, "Enough, no more.
Our work is done in Hades' maze."
The last cage will judder and rise. Then we pass through that open door
And will be blessed with those scents of Spring.

D. Hollows

39. NATIONALISATION

Nationalisation officially took place on the 1st January, 1947. Control of the industry was now transferred to the National Coal Board.

New rules and regulations which would benefit the miners were introduced and to celebrate this momentous event, the N.C.B. flag was flown from pit-heads throughout the land.

Playing it safe

One of the rules concerned the payment of compensation to the families of employees who had the misfortune to die on colliery premises. They would receive a monetary grant to help pay for funeral expenses.

The shift over, a group of miners assembled outside the pitgate waiting for the bus to take them home. Suddenly and without any warning, one of the men fainted. The others rushed to help him.

As he came round, someone asked, "Are tha all reet, George?"

"Think so," came the reply.

"But tha can do us a favour."

"Wha's that?" a collier queried.

"Drag us back into t'pit-yard, just in case."

R. Fishwick, Astley Green Colliery

N.C.B. Flag.

E TENEBRIS LUX

A stirring breeze, then a gentle fluttering,
A happy throng and a growing muttering
And a proud standard heralds brave men's freedom.
The clapping and cheering is stirring and fulsome.

Years of denial, pain, toil, sweat and tears,
Absorbed by a standard that soaks up their fears.
Yet can it erase sad thoughts of the past?
With one accord, we pray it will last.

The journey was long for them and for others.
Now, united they stand, brothers with brothers.
Dare one hope that the future is bright?
It must be so for from darkness comes light.

D. Hollows

40. CHILDREN OF THE MINES

One finds it difficult to envisage the extreme suffering of women and children, some as young as five years, who once worked in the mines. For them, it was an accepted way of life. To us, an obscenity and an abomination.

It is little wonder then that in such hazardous conditions, there were numerous casualties. Their work which denied them access to sunlight and fresh air, undermined their systems and with weakened immunity, many succumbed to the diseases of the time.

Usually, these children came from mining stock and those who survived continued in the family tradition. Even so, after years of exposure to lethal dust which corroded the lungs, a large number faced premature death.

It is fortunate that the deep concerns of well-intentioned people were voiced and noted and with the introduction of the Factory Acts, the employment of children underground was prohibited. It was a turning point in mining history.

Sadly, enforcement came too late for many but it was reassuring to know that their successors would be saved from the same fate. Now they would not be deprived of the simple pleasures of childhood, so essential to the development of maturing minds and bodies.

This short verse is a tribute to those children who paid a high price in man's pursuit of 'black diamonds'.

CHILDREN OF THE MINES

In caverns deep there is no sun
For children who slave where coal is won.
Frail frames shoring the work of men,
So near to that furnace, the Devil's den.

Above lie pastures and air so fresh
But entombed, we strive in the clawing mesh
Of darkness, danger, toil and tears.
Is this our lot for future years?

Mother Nature holds her sway.
Will we greet another day?
Our blood-stained hours are long and drear
And we are torn by endless fear.

Oft, restless earth engulfs a friend.
Can sad remembrance ever end,
For poor young souls, now here, now gone,
On whom God's gift of life once shone?

We seek but a touch of childhood joys,
Blessing our kind, both girls and boys.
Yet, these man chooses to deny.
Pray answer us. Why, oh, why?

One day, history will unfold the truth
And revere all those who lost their youth.
Then our saviours will decree
An end to bondage and set us free.

D. Hollows

41. MY PAL, BILLY

People were tiring of a conflict that seemed interminable. I had lost family members and friends as had some of my underground colleagues. As we sat to eat our snap. Eric commented, "Eh, lad, did tha know that they're beginnin' t'exchange prisoners-of-war now? That's a reet good sign. One o' my mates came 'ome last week."

"How was he?" I asked.

"A wreck," he answered. "Looks terrible an' all."

His statement was touching and I felt that I, too, needed to recount my tale to a sympathetic ear.

"Funny you mentioned that," I said. "A pal of mine came home a couple of days ago. I called on him yesterday."

"What state was 'e in then?" asked Eric.

"Much the same as your friend," I replied and went on, "Billy was a born athlete. We more or less grew up together. Sportswise, he was first-class. When, as youngsters, we raced through the fields, he'd finished before the rest of us had started. He was never caught when we played 'Leavo' and when it came to marbles, he was so skilful that he used to clear us out."

"Sounds like 'e were a talented lad," Eric observed.

"True," I agreed. "He and I used to attend the local gym, twice a week and within a few months, he was entitled to wear a proficiency vest with red piping, an honour to which we all aspired. He was a born leader and marshalled our little gang of juniors."

"A gang, eh?" Eric noted. "E'er get in trouble then?"

"Now and again," I answered. Our actions were not really malicious. We used to tap at people's windows or knock on front-doors and run off. Billy was so fast that he was never caught but some of us were so slow that we were grabbed by the occupants and after receiving a verbal warning, were cuffed round the ears for good measure. "Don't seem to 'ave done thee much 'arm," interposed Eric. "What else did you lot get up to then?" "Well," I replied," When we were about ten, Billy decided that we should go scrumping apples. A nearby orchard was full of crab-apple trees and to all intents and purposes, the large house to which it belonged was derelict. We felt that there couldn't be much harm in doing a spot of harvesting. We helped one another scale the high wall and dropped into the grounds. Everything seemed to be going well. Apples were passed to Billy who deposited them into a large bag. Suddenly, from the shade of a tree, a voice said, "Boys, if you really wanted some apples, you should have knocked at the front door. You would have been welcome to have as many as you wished." With one accord, we stared through the shafts of sunlight at a motionless figure and were shocked to see that it was a nun dressed in a black habit. Her gentle tone filled us with guilt and remorse. Quickly, we dropped our apples and made good our escape over the convent wall. Billy had already disappeared and that was the last we saw of him for almost a week. They say 'What goes round, comes round' and never have truer words been spoken for the poor lad was laid up with a severe case of colic.

The years passed and war broke out. Billy joined the Army and was sent to North Africa. Later, we learned that he had been captured by the Germans and then handed over to the Italians and found himself confined in a prisoner-of-war camp in Italy. Whilst there, some of the captives were directed to various factories where they were compelled to help produce weapons of war.

It was generally agreed among them that they were not prepared to manufacture goods which could be used against the Allies and they decided that a little sabotage was called for. Unfortunately, their non-compliance was discovered by a guard and they were promptly returned to the camp. Several days later, the prisoners were mustered into the compound. The commandant warned them that any repetition would merit severe punishment. "This is how we treat the youngest member among you," he shouted. Imagine what we are prepared to do to the older ones." Billy was then marched out, tied to a post, stripped to the waist and severely beaten.

"What were it like meetin' up wi' 'im again?" asked Eric.

"Very, very sad," I replied. The lively youngster I had once known was gone. His pale, grey face was lined and he sat in a chair, staring into space. I tried to make conversation with him but he responded by nodding and shaking his head. With tears in my eyes, I looked aghast at his mother who had given me an account of his experience. She looked down at her son and said," Come on, Billy, lift up your shirt and let Derek see your back." This he did ever so slowly, wincing at every move.

"What did tha see?" Eric questioned.

"Something I never want to see again," I replied. "Criss crossed from shoulders to waist were massive weals of every hue. Obviously, metal-tips had been attached to the whip for the cuts were the depth of ones finger." Before leaving, I ruffled his hair and mumbled, "You'll soon be all right, Billy. One day, we'll go scrumping crab-apples again."

At that, there was a slight flicker of recognition, followed by a wry smile but not a word was spoken. I felt in my heart that Billy was a broken man but hoped that the smile augured well for the future.

"That's a sad story," said Eric. "My mate's just t'same."

"And how many more?" I asked. "Must be thousands like them."

"Aye, lad," he agreed. "As they say, 'But for t'grace o' God, there go I'."

Then we went back to our work, with each of us counting his blessings.

A BROKEN MAN

A broken man with a broken heart,
The debris of conflict and youth bled dry.
Body and spirit now torn apart.
Surely, Heaven itself must mourn and cry.

Dear Lord, we ask for your outpouring love,
God's gracious gift to all creation,
And compassionate mercy that comes from above,
Granting peace, perfect peace to every nation.

D. Hollows

42. ANOTHER DIMENSION

The shift over, Josh and I sat in the pit-canteen. Soon, we were joined by Horace, a collier.

"You know", remarked Josh as he stirred his tea." Life's really strange.

"So's women," Horace interrupted. "If tha thinks life's strange, tha wants t'come to my house. My missus goes strange when I take a couple of bob out of me wages for t'bookie's."

"What's brought this on?" I asked Josh.

"Well, last night, I was reading a book on the supernatural and it made me think."

"Tha's gettin' maudlin, lad. Buck up, will tha. Won't catch me readin' stuff like that," Horace stated.

"I understand your meaning," I assured Josh. "You mean strange in the sense that there doesn't seem to be any logical explanation when certain events occur."

"Exactly," he agreed.

"What I am about to tell you will certainly make you think," I said and I recounted an incident which had happened several years previously.

A friend of mine, Gail, became a W.A.A.F. In 1940, at the height of the Battle of Britain, she was posted to a fighter-station. Her function was that of clerk in the debriefing room. Her close friend, Dorothy, worked alongside her and was engaged to Neil, a young pilot. Upon returning from sorties, the airmen made a point of tapping at the window, waving to the girls and entering the adjoining door to make their reports. On one particular day, there was much activity over the Channel. Some time elapsed before the first aircraft landed, followed at intervals, by several others. Most of them bore the scars of aerial combat.

Standing at the window, Gail looked out over the field. Suddenly, her vision was blocked by an approaching figure who smiled and waved to her. She reciprocated and observed that he was carrying his flying-helmet and that he was soaking wet.

"Neil's back," she called across the room.

Dorothy locked up and waved to her fiance. "Thank goodness he's safe," she remarked.

Expectantly, the two girls awaited Neil's entrance but they were disappointed. "Hang on," Gail advised and she stepped outside. The earth was bathed in sunlight and there wasn't a sign of rain. "Not a soul in sight," she confirmed.

For a time, there was a stillness in the room. No one spoke. Two Spitfires landed. On this occasion, the pilots disregarded the customary ritual and entered immediately.

Looking at Dorothy, one said, "I am so sorry to tell you that Neil didn't make it. He went down in the Channel. We've been circling round for ages but there's no sign of him."

Like so many young men, Neil had sacrificed his young life to defend our island and to thwart enemy invasion.

As in the de-briefing room, there was a short silence at our table. Josh looked at Horace.

"There is more in heaven and in earth, Horatio, than man ever dreamed of in his philosophy," he concluded. A very apt quotation, I felt.

FOOTNOTE

As a member of the Battle of Britain Historical Society, I recently spoke to Gail who lives in retirement on the South coast. Now in her late eighties, and with the experience of Neil's mysterious appearance still fresh in her mind, she devotes her time to tracing, wherever possible, the whereabouts of airmen reported missing over six decades ago.

43. PER ARDUA AD ASTRA
PILOT OFFICER DONALD SMITH
– ANOTHER OF THE FEW

Donald flew with 616 Squadron (Spitfires), based at Leconfield.

During a night-flying exercise on the 7th August, 1940, he was forced to abandon his aircraft which crashed and exploded. He sustained injuries which required a period of convalescence and returned home to Highley, Shropshire.

Whilst recuperating, he visited a local hostelry run by Mrs. Bache. He was invited into the private quarters for a drink. Their conversation was interrupted by a radio bulletin announcing that there had been heavy bombing by the Luftwaffe. Donald thanked Mrs. Bache for her hospitality and added that he intended to return to his duties forthwith. Mrs. Bache advised him that in view of the nature of his injuries, he might not be fit enough to fly. Donald replied that too many pilots were being shot down and that every available man was needed to confront the attackers.

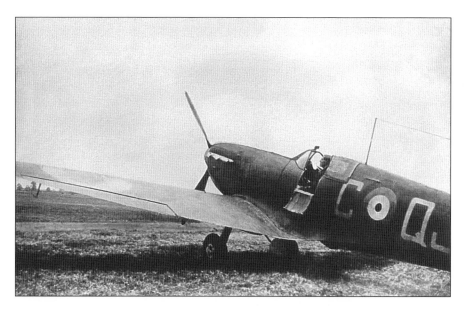

Flying Officer Donald S. Smith (616 South Yorkshire Squadron.)

On the 27th September, 1940, flying from Duxford and acting as Squadron "weaver", he was mortally wounded in combat. He died the following day and now rests in St. Mary's Churchyard, Highley.

Donald had been a schoolmaster and taught under the direction of his father, Major F. Smith who was Head of the local school. Upon completion of my teacher training, the latter offered me a post which I was very privileged to accept and for some time, I lived with the family.

"Never in the field of human conflict, was so much owed by so many to so few" (Winston Churchill).

DEDICATED TO THE MEMORY OF
FLYING OFFICER DONALD S.SMITH
(616 SPITFIRE SQUADRON)

Young Donald, schoolmaster, a man of grace,
Steadfast, determined and seeking his place:
First in the R.A.F. and then with the Fleet
And back to the former, his mission complete.

Angry clouds loom overhead,
Peace in our time hangs by a thread.
Then bugles sound a call to arms
But the fearless Few help abate alarms.

His craft spins down on a training flight,
Exploding on impact. Don survives that night,
Save injured legs, nursed and welcome leave:
Home to his roots. Too early to grieve. .

Amid chatter, the clatter of pint-pots and plates,
In his favourite local, his tale he relates.
Yet as he speaks, the news brings frowns.
There's a heavy raid on one of our towns.

"We are fast losing pilots, so it's back to base."
Against landlady's advice, he packs his case.
Off to 616 where he joins his friends,
To wage war against evil. The stress never ends.

From Duxford, as "weaver", ninth month of the year,
Tidings the village is fearful to hear.
Shot down, sore-wounded, he passed on the next day.
For him and for others, so many did pray.

In St. Mary's, Highley, he finds his rest
And eternal peace. He has done his best.
With undaunted spirit and heart so brave,
For you and for me, his life he gave.

His name is revered forevermore,
With his comrades who entered God's Heavenly door.
Their honour is etched in the skies above,
For they winged as eagles and gifted a dove.

D. Hollows

44. AS FATE DECREES

The war was virtually at an end. Germany had surrendered.

"Glad it's nearly all o' er," remarked a collier as we descended in the cage.

"Only t'Japs to beat now," replied Barney and looking at me, he added. "An' tha'll be able to get back to thy studies again." I nodded in agreement but I couldn't help thinking of those poor unfortunates who were still caught up in the Far East conflict. Among them were some of my friends and neighbours. I thought of the traumas they must have experienced and of the suffering they must have witnessed. Several years later, I was to learn at first-hand from a survivor.

Before the war and for more than twenty years, Kathleen lived in Singapore. During that time she had run a race-course, owned a dress-shop and been a companion-tutor in the home of a Chinese business-man.

In 1942, as the Japanese marched on the city, she became a Red Cross worker and helped to evacuate the sick and wounded. Shortly afterwards, she boarded the S.S. Kuala which was full of evacuees, men, women and children. Within minutes, the vessel received three direct hits. An officer, brandishing a revolver, gave the instruction to abandon ship. Although she could not swim, Kathleen hadn't any choice other than to obey. Her hands were burned raw as she slid down the rope. Once in the water, she was able to float by cupping her arms round the slats of a wooden bath-mat that drifted by. Very soon, she climbed on to a raft, which had been thrown from the S.S. Kuala. For several hours, wave after wave of Japanese aircraft bombed and machine-gunned those in the water. As she put it, the sea turned red with blood and was covered in dead fish and floating bodies.

Eventually, they were rescued by the crew of an Indonesian fishing-ship who demanded their valuables before taking them on board. Disembarking on a small island, they were introduced to the headman who supplied them with food and water but pointed out that they could not stay. Japanese justice, if one were caught housing the enemy, was swift and brutal. He then gave them a small sailing vessel and optimism returned only to be dashed when they landed on an island which, unknown to them, was occupied by Japanese troops.

As prisoners, they were transported to Sumatra and for the next three months she was imprisoned with ten other British women in a small garage. It was here that Kathleen sustained an injury which left her with a permanent limp. A guard attempted to assault a young female. Kathleen leapt to her defence and hurled herself on the sentry who smashed her feet with the butt of his rifle. This incident was reported to the commandant who promised to deal severely with the offender. He was transferred from his duties outside the garage but as he was seen undertaking other tasks in the area, it was apparent that the assurance had not been honoured and that the matter had been regarded lightly.

Captivity in a civil prison followed. Along with the other women, Kathleen was marched into the jungle and forced to cut down trees to make an air-strip. Their diet consisted of a mug of rice or sago flour. These daily excursions gave them the opportunity to collect the roots of edible plants, which they hid about their persons until they returned to their quarters. Among them, were Dutch nuns who, with their wide-sleeved habits, were able to smuggle in plentiful supplies of dietary supplements.

In those squalid conditions, the regime was harsh and unforgiving but amidst the misery and gloom, there was a glimmer of hope. Fate had decreed that an enemy should become a friend and man's essential goodness shone through the darkness of despair. It came in the shape of an elderly Japanese sentry who, out of sight of the other guards and at great risk to himself, performed many acts of human kindness. He was at his happiest when he handed round photographs of his wife and smiling children whom he had been compelled to leave behind in Nagasaki. One day, in broken English, he observed, "That fella Churchill, he very good man. He number one. He come soon and you all go home."

Failure to bow to a guard warranted a severe beating but at least, the commanding officer allowed the prisoners. to participate in weekly religious services, The ceremony was conducted by a priest from an adjoining camp which housed male prisoners. Unknown to their captors, the men had concealed a radio in one of the huts. Accordingly, the chants were often interspersed with news bulletins concerning the progress of the war.

In 1945, it was clear that the Allies were winning. Fearing final retribution, the commandant put on a display of generosity and it wasn't long before several lorries laden with supplies, rolled into the compound. There was great joy as the crates were opened but with the euphoria came tragedy. A young Indian girl was so ravenous that she swallowed several raw eggs in quick succession. Her digestive system could not cope with the sudden change. Within minutes, she collapsed and died in front of her friends. This cast a huge shadow over the proceedings.

The announcement that hostilities had ended was made by a group of male prisoners who walked unmolested by the sentries, into the women's quarters.

After delousing, Kathleen's first thought was to relax in a hot bath, a luxury she was able to enjoy when she was flown back to Singapore and billeted in an hotel. Her weight had gone down from 11st. 4lb. to 5st. 12lb, but somehow she had survived.

For this brave woman, the journey to Sydney and then to England and home was filled with memories. In a changing world there was much to do, a new life to face. The past was over – or was it? Her eyes told me that it could never really be so.

45. LEST WE FORGET

During World War Two, a friend of mine was a muleteer in the Burmese jungle and he often spoke of the doggedness and courage of his charges with whom he developed a close rapport. Other family members and friends on active service also referred to the sterling work performed by a wide variety of animals, including horses, dogs, elephants, carrier pigeons and cats.

Latterly, some deservedly received tangible recognition for their contribution but during history's many conflicts, countless unrecorded names would have been lost, honoured in memory only by their handlers, owners and those whose lives they had saved.

We must never forget the animals serving on the Home Front in the darkness of the mine. On occasion, canaries were used to detect lethal gases which when identified, could be neutralised, thus averting the possibility of explosion with its catastrophic consequences. Several centuries ago, mice and even dogs were used for this very same purpose. The rugged, little pit-ponies also played a vital role. They worked extremely hard in harsh conditions, slipping and stumbling along the tramways as they drew the laden tubs. They were tough and they were loyal. There is a recorded incident of a miner's having been cast into total darkness when his lamp was accidentally extinguished. Sensing his unenviable predicament, the pony allowed his keeper to hold on to his tail and led the way through pitch-black tunnels until they emerged into the light and eventual safety.

From time to time, the pit-ponies were rested. Initially blinkered so that their eyes would not be damaged by sunlight, they surfaced and were taken to nearby fields where they revelled in their new-found freedom by galloping and prancing through the pastures. It is reassuring to know that, in retirement, they maintained contact with the miners who regularly visited them bearing gifts, usually in the shape of sliced apples.

In these pages, I consider it fitting to pay tribute to our unsung animal heroes throughout the centuries. From them, we can learn so much. Their sacrifices should never be forgotten and should be an inspiration to us all.

LEST WE FORGET

Thrust into a cauldron forged in Hell,
Innocence destroyed by gas, shot and shell:
Steadfast and loyal through darkened days,
Sacrificed by mortals' errant ways.

In spite of all, we served our masters,
Bidding farewell to peace: now courting disasters.
On fields of death, under angry skies,
Obscenities drowned our anguished cries.

We asked so little of you, our friends
But betrayed we felt. Can you make amends?
Expecting nought save lasting love
And the joys conceived in realms above.

We gave our all in freedom's name.
Should man now hang his head in shame?
Such horrors are born of human weakness.
Learn from us. Embrace our meekness.

Do not grieve. We played our part.
Just remember us with gladdened heart.
So many entered that Heavenly door,
Your faithful friends, the debris of war.

We now bathe in the glow of pain's release
And rest evermore in Eternal Peace.
There is hope that our Lord's simple message brings:
Pray honour and revere all living things.

D. Hollows

46. A HEALING HAND

Although the war was over, I was still serving as a Bevin Boy. During several days' respite from my underground duties, I made a sombre visit to France.

On a warm, sunny Sunday afternoon, I laid flowers on my cousin Fred's grave in Bayeux, Normandy. As a member of a tank crew, he had lost his life during the bloody battle for Caen. With my own sad and private thoughts, I surveyed the many headstones which marked the resting-places of countless young men whose lives had been cut short. I despised the dreadful waste and human suffering caused by man's errant proclivities. Experiencing a gamut of mixed emotions, mainly of sorrow and intense anger at the injustice of it all, I could feel only bitterness toward our former enemies.

Bayeux Military Cemetery,
Normandy (where a cousin rests).

One month later, a friend of mine who was an army captain, invited me to a camp housing German prisoners-of-war. With an ending of hostilities, repatriation was being implemented. Now, at long last, I was able to come face to face with some of our late adversaries.

As I entered the recreation-room, my attention was drawn to an imposing figure standing by a window. He was over six feet tall, broad-shouldered, with fair hair and clear blue eyes. "So this is the typical Nazi," I mused. As he approached me, he extended his hand in greeting which I reluctantly accepted. In excellent English, he introduced himself. "Good afternoon, I am Hans," he said. I reciprocated, "Derek", I replied. It is amazing that after many years, I still recall the gist of our conversation. "I am so glad that the fighting is over," he commented. "Now I can return to my wife and children."

"You are very lucky," I said. "Three of my cousins and some of my friends will never return."

"Yes, I am fortunate and I am so sorry," he replied with obvious sincerity. "I, too, have lost family members. War is dreadful and I hate it."

"Where are you from?" I asked.

"Saxony," he answered. "As a matter of fact, I am as English as you," he laughed and continued, "For all we know, we may be related. It is said that in the First World War, Saxon soldiers rarely served in the front-line against the British."

"And what of your family?" I queried.

"I will show you," he responded and I noticed a tear running down his cheek. He produced a photograph of his pretty wife and three smiling children. Although he had been spared, I appreciated that they too, must also have been affected by his long absence, "And this is the front view of my house," he added and handed me a second photograph. It had two mullioned bay windows and I saw that there was a sign over the door.

"Very cosy," I observed "Is it a shop of some sort?"

"Yes, indeed," he answered. "I cannot wait to open it up again."

"What do you sell?" I questioned.

"Toys and things," he advised. "And I am the village toy maker," he declared proudly. "Before the war, I would go into the woods to collect timber, season it and then carve it into toys and souvenirs. My main customers were holiday-makers who wished to buy mementoes of their visit. I hope it won't be too long before they come back again."

"Obviously, you enjoy your work," I said.

"I certainly do," he replied. "It is such a peaceful job. I did not wish to go to war. I hate fighting but had I refused, I would have been shot as would so many others."

Deep down, I sensed that these were not false utterances and as I warmed to him, I felt that my initial anger was beginning to dissipate. I became only too well aware that continued bitterness can be self-destructive. As with so many others, he had been compelled to participate in a hostile and obscene activity that was completely alien to his nature. I looked at him and recalled my father's account of the Christmas, 1914, truce when the carol 'Silent Night' echoed across No Man's Land and when, for a fleeting moment, enemies became brothers. No doubt, I could have met others in that camp who held much more extreme views but it had not been intended. I had been fortunate enough to touch the healing hand of a good man and I knew that my family and friends who lay in foreign fields, would have felt the same.

We bade our farewells and parted company. I did not see Hans again but I was consoled and happy in the knowledge that he would return to his village and surrounded by his wife, children and his beloved toys, the peace that radiated from him would reflect in the hearts of others.

RECONCILIATION

I met an unknown in a quiet place.
The conflict over and new-found gladness.
We looked at each other, face to face
But my ire-blemished heart was full of sadness.

The stranger approached with open hand.
Yet still rank bitterness and much regret
For one who had coveted our precious land
And I remembered lost friends and could not forget.

With gentle voice, he spoke to me.
There seemed sharp awareness of my plight.
Then came a picture of his family
And I noted a blurring of his sight.

Tear-drops ran from clear, blue eyes.
I felt some compassion, some concern.
Anger consumes. 'tis so unwise
And I sensed there was yet more to learn.

"My wife and children here, you see?"
Nodding, I smiled to give him strength.
"In Saxony, they wait for me."
And our discourse continued at length.

"All war I hate. I had no choice
And I am so sorry for your friends.
It is over now. Let us rejoice.
May God grant we make amends.

I have a little village store,"
He added with growing pride and poise.
Pray tell me then a little more.
"Why, I spend all my time making toys.

In a toy-maker's world, there are so many joys
And I breathe in the peace my craft brings,
Seen in the eyes of young girls and boys.
Then Heaven above me smiles and sings."

I felt my anger fading away,
For a truly blessed man I had met.
Such memories will always stay
Of a righteous soul one will never forget.

D. Hollows

47. KISMET

When I went to college to undertake my teacher-training, I was surprised to find that I was the only ex-Bevin Boy in the group. My associates and several of my tutors had served in various branches of the armed forces, both in this country and overseas. Some had seen action. Indeed, our Student President, an unassuming Welsh boy, had commanded a midget submarine.

My first year room-mate, Don, a navigator, had been engaged in dropping supplies to our troops in Burma. He had been awarded a Croix de Guerre. When approached by an inquisitive eighteen year old who broached the subject, Don replied, "Well, they sent us a couple of medals to dish out. Not enough for everybody, so we drew straws. That's about it."

I befriended Neil, an ex-R.A.F. navigator. He was a sober, serious-minded young man in his twenties. Often, he appeared to be lost deep in his own thoughts.

One evening, as we sat in the canteen drinking coffee, Neil looked at me and said, "War's a funny thing. Look at us, here now. Why are we here? Why am I here?"

"Well ," I replied. "We were lucky enough to get through this war in one piece. Now we want to do something with our lives. Give the world a little of what is good and constructive and what better place to start than with the young."

"I agree," he said. "But I wonder why me? Certainly, I want to teach and I'll do my best." He continued, "Someone else could have been here instead of me."

"Who?" I asked.

"Some of my pals who didn't make it. A few of them wanted to be teachers after it was all over but they never got the chance. They were a great bunch of lads," he replied.

"Do you know, Neil," I said. "Sometimes, I ask myself that question too. I suppose many of us who survived the war feel the same."

He paused for a moment then said, "Life's strange. I had a very weird experience in the R.A.F." and he began his story.

"We were down for a bombing run deep into Germany. It was dusk. We left the briefing-room and went to our transport. We climbed aboard. We knew that we were going to have a pretty rough time of it, what with the German ack-ack and the night-fighters. Believe me, we were worried all right and damned scared. As our truck drew on to the runway, we noticed a Lancaster on the grass verge. I wondered what it was doing there. The cockpit light was on and we could see its markings quite clearly. The pilot was looking directly at us. He had a broad grin on his face and he kept giving us the thumbs-up sign. We all waved back. We reached our 'plane. The engines were turning over. Suddenly, our skipper looked at us. His face blanched. 'See whose 'plane that was' he said. 'It was Tony's. He went down a couple of days ago with his crew.' It was as if an icy hand had touched us. We took off, wondering what on earth was going on. To cut a long story short, we completed our mission and returned safely.

"Later, we approached some of the ground-crew. I asked them what the Lanc. was doing off the runway and even mentioned the markings. One of the lads replied, 'There hasn't been a 'plane sir. None at all.'"

Neil went on, "We were all shocked. We talked it over in the mess and concluded that Tony was still with us in spirit. Somehow, he knew that we would make it and he was letting us know. You ever had on experience like that?" he asked.

"Yes", I replied, "Though not quite the same as yours" and I recounted the incident when I was trapped by a roof-fall on the coalface. I continued, "I was in a very confined space, completely unable to see. The thick dust made breathing difficult. I really believed that my number was up but I felt that I was not alone. I cannot explain it but I was aware of caring and concerned entities at my side. After some effort, my work-mates got me out. It was an incident that I can never forget."

Neil nodded. He understood only too well. We finished our drinks and returned to our rooms to continue our studies. There was still much to learn if we were to implement the wishes of Neil's lost friends and to honour their sacrifice.

48. DISTANT VOICES

Recently, I read a short article on Roman Britain and I was reminded of my early years when a study of our nation's history formed an important part of the school curriculum. I recalled that my class-mates and I enthused over countless colourful events from various eras but generally speaking, nothing inspired us more than the period when the mighty Roman Empire ruled all.

In vivid imagination, we marvelled at the thought of disciplined legions marching along the straight, drained roads that were their creation, perhaps to engage in battle or to transfer to a fortification or settlement. Learning about their system of government, their beliefs and rituals, occupations, interests and strategic planning in war and peace stirred our boyish enthusiasm. To us, they were a race apart and so well advanced in their time.

In our unpredictable climate, the unearthing of coal proved to be a blessing. Initially, they were bewitched by the gleaming, black rock which they fashioned into trinkets but they also knew that it was combustible and that it could create heat and energy for domestic and industrial purposes. It was invaluable to their tradesmen and especially so to their blacksmiths, upon whom they placed great reliance.

Leisure activities included visits to their baths where they relaxed in the piped, hot water. Little did they realise that their inventiveness would, in future years, be modified and enjoyed by those whose homes now have central-heating.

Legionaries, many of whom came from warmer climes and manning outposts in some of the more environmentally hostile areas, would have welcomed the warmth of the firelight glow. Indeed, traces of the burnt fuel have been found on various sites.

Our ex-Bevin Boys will surely feel an affinity with those who, in early times, mined the coal. From their own experiences, they will appreciate the toil involved and the hazards that faced all who worked beneath the surface.

Most importantly, we must acknowledge the contribution that the Romans made to our language, much of which derives from Latin roots. As a matter of interest, I have compiled a list of words based on the mining theme. It provides an insight into the development of our tongue, the legacy of a long-lost empire which was destined to destroy itself.

DISTANT VOICES

coal	carbo	disaster	calamitas
block and tackle	trochlea	lamp	lucerna
mine	metallum	prayers	preces
pony	mannus	God	Deus
surface	superficies	clog	sculponeae
mouse, rat	mus	courage	fortitudo
daylight	dies	pickaxe	dolabra
toil	labor	injury	vulnus
underground	subterraneus	spade	pala
sweat	sudor	stretcher	leticula
darkness	tenebrae	shovel	rutrum
output	fructus	doctor	medicus
shaft, pit	pureus	wooden beam	trabs, lignum
conversation	sermo	nurse	nutrix
tunnel	cuniculus	wood, timber	materia
wit, humour	facetiae	give first aid to	ad tempus mederi
ventilation	perfiare	chain	catena
thirsty	sitiens	bath	balneum
arch	arcus	machine, engine	machina
water	aqua	wage	merces
heat	calor	meal	cibus
to drink	bibere	to eat	edere
rock	saxum	tired	lassus
hunger	fames	rest	requies
unstable	instabilis	to sleep	dormire
snack	cenula		
miner	fossor		
dust	pulvis		
conscript	tiro		
gas	vapor		
workmate	collega		
danger	periculum		
comrade	socius		
caution	cautio		
craftsman	faber		
explosion	fragor		
blacksmith	ferrarius		

49. A TIMELY REMINDER TO ALL
EX-BEVIN BOYS

Jimmy's Bevin Boy days were long past. One night, there was a knock at the front door which was opened by a grey haired old man.

"Excuse me, but art tha Jimmy Smith, once a Bevin Boy?" asked the visitor.

"Yes," came the reply.

"At last, I've found thee. Thowt tha were a goner," said the man.

"Had trouble finding me?" Jimmy questioned.

"Can say that again. Been all o' er t'place lookin' for thee," announced the visitor.

"Well, now you've found me," said Jimmy.

"Aye, that's reet. Tha knows, we 'ad lads down t'pit diggin' for thee for years. Wore out a few shovels an' all."

"But I left the mine some time ago," Jimmy assured him.

"'appen tha did but afore tha left, tha forgot t' and in thy tally an' I've come t'collect it."

BROTHERS

Wheresoe'er on this globe the miner toils,
He is bound by a chain of endless coils
To a brotherhood forged through bad times and good,
Tempered by friendship, courage and blood.

Common the dangers encountered each day
But humour and laughter their fears do allay.
Deep down in the blackness amid rock and coal,
Oft-times, Nature extracts a terrible toll.

Be proud of those men, resolute and strong,
Salt of the earth and have been so for long.
They know what is important, what matters most:
So to miners worldwide please offer a toast.

They treasure so well God's great gift of life.
Those who have been there have no time for strife.
They decry man's greed and pray wars will cease.
Through them, we may find everlasting Peace.

D. Hollows

50. RUTH'S POEMS

Ruth Batchelor and her mother, Joyce, are both members of the Bevin Boys' Association. Ruth's father, Alan, who sadly passed away in 1993, was a Bevin Boy based at Chesterfield and Bolsover.

During their first visit to an Association reunion of the Norfolk Branch, they were deeply moved by some of the stories recounted by various members. This prompted Ruth to write "Bevin Boys." It is a poignant composition which refers to the "Forgotten Men" who, initially, did not receive any recognition for their service to Crown and Country.

For many years, the Bevin Boys were, as a group, excluded from the annual Cenotaph March-past and it would appear that this was due to their not having served in the Armed Forces.

However, in 1998, a motion was passed in the House of Commons granting them representation in the Parade so that they too, might pay homage to their war dead.

On the strength of this, Ruth was commissioned by the Bevin Boys' Association Committee to produce an updated version of "Bevin Boys", which resulted in the production of "Bevin Boys 2."

The poem acknowledges the shift in attitude and expresses the sentiments of those who served underground. It also mentions the Albert Hall Service of Remembrance. Currently, the Bevin Boys are not allowed to participate but one hopes that with the passing of time, long-overdue acceptance will be confirmed and members of the "Forgotten Army" will assume their rightful place.

BEVIN BOYS 1

No Hats, No Plumes,
No Uniforms,
No Badge for them to wear.
No Regiment,
No choice
No Recognition.

No light, No sight,
No chance to fight,
No Medal for Defence,
No Honours' Roll,
No bugle call,
No acknowledgement.

The cage, the hole,
The dreaded drop,
The deepest Trench Foxhole.
In seams of eighteen inches high
They dug the precious coal.

On hands and knees
Like rats they crawled,
In pit-falls, were entombed,
The dust, the dirt,
Now, feelings hurt,
Continued blackness looms.

But still, No Hats,
Or uniforms,
No Badge or Medal Proud
The Bevin Boys, Forgotten Men,
Remembrance, Not Allowed.

Ruth Batchelor

BEVIN BOYS 2

The Bevin Boys' Campaign moves on....
They're acknowledged at long last
And in '98, so proud they were
At the Remembrance Day March Past.

On that cold and damp November morn,
They assembled one and all,
In helmets white, with heads held high,
They parade along Whitehall.

The Cenotaph, their focal point,
With emotions hard to hide,
They marched with other Servicemen
For their comrades who had died.

But still the recognition needs
to meet the public eye,
The final goal, the Albert Hall,
Their Banner flying high.

The Service of Remembrance,
The Honour and Respect,
The Bevin Boys are part of this,
When our heads are bowed, reflect.

Ruth Batchelor

51. BEVIN BOYS' MEDALS

Comparatively recently, as ex-Bevin Boys, we learned that we are entitled to wear medals (non gratis), for our services. Currently, the Government is considering the feasibility of awarding a badge of honour. Such tardiness emphasises our being termed the 'Forgotten Army'.

Acceptable as they are, their true significance lies in the golden memories they evoke of enduring friendships formed so long ago.

Without exception, we regard such honours as a tribute to the miners with whom we served and who did not receive any recognition for their invaluable contribution.

52. A RACE APART

In these pages, references have been made to the stoicism and courage of the miners.

Sadly, those with whom I worked, Barney, Steve, Paddy, Jimmy, Tom, George and Spurge, not forgetting so many others with whom I associated, are now long gone but while men continue to labour in the bowels of the earth, they will always be remembered. With the passing of time, their toil-stained faces may become blurred and their names obscure but they symbolised the virtues of men who were a race apart and about whom so little is known by those who are not acquainted with the structure and fabric of mining communities. They belonged to a vast, world-wide brotherhood and during their life span, were vital contributors to our nation's wealth and, indeed, to our survival at a critical period in our history.

For a fleeting moment, I was privileged to have been but one small part of the fraternity and for that, I am eternally grateful.

I witnessed their achievements, often against seemingly overwhelming odds and indulged in their humour which carried them through the good days and the bad. They were elements in an on-going process which could tax man's endurance to its limits and displayed unbelievable heroism which was rarely recorded in print but certainly appreciated by their colleagues.

In 1946, I was involved in a roof-fall on the coalface. Three colliers with whom I was working at the time, risked their own lives to save mine. Plaudits were not sought. A sincere "Thank you, lads" sufficed. For such fine men of muscle, sinew, sweat and great humility, the satisfaction of knowing that a comrade's life had been saved was reward enough.

53. BOTELER BOYS (Deus Spes Nostra)

During my secondary school-days, the names of a well-respected master who had perished with the sinking of H.M.S. Hood and several ex-Boteler pupils who had been lost on active service were announced in morning assemblies. It wasn't until after my period of service underground was completed that I discovered the true cost of the conflict. The list of casualties had increased considerably.

Those boys were my friends and companions, so young, so vibrant and eagerly anticipating a future which was cruelly and abruptly denied them. Had they survived, the sterling qualities of character-building nurtured and embraced through their Boteler training would undoubtedly have contributed to the healing of a tired world emerging from six dark years of war.

We who knew them remember them with pride and trust that future generations will learn to appreciate their sacrifice.

ROLL OF HONOUR
(BOTELER GRAMMAR SCHOOL, WARRINGTON, 1939-1945)

E.G. BISHOP

J.S. BLUNT

H.M. BOARDMAN

G. CHAPPELL

E. COLTON

C. DAINTITH

J.S. DAVIES

E.W. GIBSON

R.S. DEIGHTON

B. FINDLEY

G.B. HALL

W.B. HAYES

J. HIGHAM

W. HOUGHTON

F.S. HUGHES

L. ISHERWOOD

F.A. LEITCH

A.B. LOMAX

M.H. McDONALD

J.R.M. MARR

E.J.M. NIXON

H.K. PASS

H. PODMORE

J.D. SAMPSON

J. SPENCER

P. WELDING

J. WILLIAMS

A.G. DANIELS

K. ABBOTT, SCHOOLMASTER (H.M.S. HOOD)
IN PROUD MEMORY

A TRIBUTE

Our Roll of Honour means much to me.
Faces long gone that I still see,
Life-flushed and filled with spirited joys:
A happy band of Boteler boys.

The School, our daily meeting-place,
Renowned for endeavour and mannerly grace.
Then darkened skies loomed overhead,
Forging doubt and growing dread.

Ken Abbott, a master, went down with the 'Hood'.
For him and for friends, in silence we stood.
His space was filled by his grieving wife
And her courage embellished his fleeting life.

Kindly Welding and Leitch, Deighton and Hall,
A smiling quartet, respected by all.
Now, one by one, there were gaps in the ranks:
On land, sea and air, they went with our thanks.

There were Hughes and Higham, Nixon and Marr
And Findley, the swimmer, who out-paced us by far,
Found his last resting-place in a corner of Greece,
With his comrades in arms. May they now rest in peace.

Edgar Colton, born athlete, a hero of mine,
The School's Victor Ludorum in '39.
From realms above he lost his life,
Sacrificed in a world of strife.

Our Roll for the fallen bears other names too,
Of boys full of promise, boys whom I knew.
Never forgotten and never afar,
They found Heaven's portals, forever ajar.

Each name had a face and a soul pure and true.
Their legacy, they now pass down to you.
One and all had a bountiful heart
And a fervent wish that you play your part.

Remembrance will help you in so many ways.
Look to the light in your darker days.
Our boys are still with you, so bathe in the glow
Of the Boteler spirit that we shared long ago.

D. Hollows

54. CONTEMPLATION

As we honour those who made the supreme sacrifice during two World Wars, it would not be amiss to remember another group of young men. They were the Bevin Boys who became known as the 'Forgotten Army'.

The work was arduous and demanding. Death or injury forever lay in the shadows. Roof-falls were frequent and the possibility of explosions which could decimate an area and human life without warning, a constant threat. In 1943, one out of every four mineworkers was either killed or injured.

For some inexplicable reason, their records were destroyed in the 1950's Only a handful were retrieved and stored for posterity. The experiment in which older, experienced miners supported by the Bevin Boys may have been regarded by some as a monumental blunder. However, the result of their joint efforts was self-evident. At no little cost, the coal had been won and peace had been declared.

Picture by courtesy of Ruth Batchelor.

Over the years, their numbers have dwindled. Those who remain are in their late 70's and 80's and take great pride in being members of the Bevin Boys' Association. Recently, they learned that they are entitled to three medals for their services.

It was a moving experience for them to see their green banner proudly borne down the Mall to commemorate the 60th Anniversary of the end of World War Two and to witness the march-past by a small group of members on Remembrance Sunday. They placed their wreath and carried their own book of remembrance past the Cenotaph in homage to their comrades.

When we bow our heads in prayer for family and friends who were lost, let us not forget all those unsung heroes who died in the dust-laden darkness of the mine over six decades ago.

55. THINK ON THIS

Since joining the association, I have in my own small way, attempted to increase our membership by submitting letters to various newspapers. Without exception, they have been only too pleased to co-operate.

The response from ex-Bevin Boys and widows has exceeded my expectations. During our discussions and in our correspondence, the past becomes vivid, vital and alive. As time passed, we trod our individual paths but through our communication, we are transported back to yesteryear. We are no longer in our seventies and eighties but in our teens again, experiencing the frustration of not being in the armed Forces and the anticipation of entering the alien world below. Large numbers of us had volunteered for military service but for various reasons, our ambitions were thwarted.

When I converse with these men, I am aware of an attitude that is unfounded and ill-deserved. I detect an initial hesitancy, almost an innate sense of guilt that they were Bevin Boys but as the rapport develops, there is a noticeable surge of excitement and memories of long ago are recalled. When Bevin Boy speaks to Bevin Boy, there is a sense of mutual sympathy and empathy and a cleansing of the wound.

There were those who appreciated our plight and because they believed and understood, no explanation was necessary. Others, by perverse reasoning or complete ignorance, preferred not to believe. For them, no explanation was possible. We, too, lost family members and dear friends and were not a race apart.

So many vulnerable teenagers were subjected to ridicule, caustic comments, even raised eyebrows at our not being in uniform. We were sensitive enough to understand what was meant and it hurt. Did they not consider that their condemnation of us reflected on generations of brave miners?

The uninitiated would do well to remember that day by day, we faced hazards in the dark and dusty world beneath us. As long as we remained underground, there might not have been a tomorrow. We were well aware that rock-falls and explosions were a constant threat but we were obliged to take our chances. Alongside our experienced mining friends, we did what was expected of us.

In life's eventide, we have fond memories of our colleagues who risked life and limb below the surface and through these reminiscences, we are regaining our dignity and self-respect. We owe much to the miners who nurtured us during those troubled times and we should not be ashamed of our contribution. No longer should we hide in the shadows but step into the light with heads held high and proudly proclaim, "I was a Bevin Boy."

MEMORIA

The pit has gone. It is no more
And one needs tap at memory's door
To recall those hectic, distant days
That changed our lives in countless ways.

From all walks we came and strode,
Brothers of toil down that dusty road,
In a darkened world beneath the ground,
Forging bonds, new friendships found.

For our mentors, this life was ever so.
We learned so much in the lamp-light glow
Of honour, courage, loyalty and then
We cast off youth and became as men.

The mine is now bereft and bare
And I can only stand and stare,
Remembering those, our long-lost hosts
As silence reigns but I hear their ghosts.

D. Hollows

POSTSCRIPT

During the years that I have recorded my memoirs, I have noted that there have been numerous mining disasters. Mexico, Siberia, America, China, Russia and Poland have all suffered losses.

We may never know just how much courage was shown in those subterranean workings but miners world-wide will appreciate that there would have been many unrecorded acts of self-sacrifice.

It is with humility and deep sincerity that miners and ex-Bevin Boys will unite in extending heartfelt sympathy to all who have been touched by mining tragedy and can assure them that those who have been lost will always he honoured by members of our fraternity.

DIALECT AND GLOSSARY

The majority of the work-force at the Lyme Colliery was drawn from Haydock, Ashton-in-Makerfield, Golborne, Earlestown and Newton-le-Willows.

The Bevin Boys who joined them were introduced not only to a world of toil but also to a new language of dialect with its variations.

Initially, interpretation of instructions could present difficulties for those who found this alternative form of speech a hindrance. The puzzled expressions on the faces of the uninitiated created a great deal of mirth among our mentors but they were understanding and compassionate men and were always prepared to enunciate slowly and with clarity. At times, the canteen and underground workings were reminiscent of class-rooms.

Some Bevin Boys absorbed these forms of expression with alacrity and spoke with surprising fluency. Indeed, had one not known better, one could have believed that they too, had been nurtured in those catchment areas. Their achievement reinforced their feeling of final acceptance and filled them with a sense of pride. After all, the miners were proud of their language and so were we for we were now virtually bi-lingual.

GLOSSARY (DIALECT EXAMPLES)

abaht	*about*	*o' er yon*	*over there*
affie	*afternoon*	*on t'*	*on the*
afore	*before*	*'ow*	*how*
ain't	*am not, are not*	*owd*	*old*
allus	*always*	*reet*	*right*
an'	*and*	*sin'*	*since*
an' a'	*as well as, also*	*sithee*	*see you, look here*
'appen	*perhaps, maybe*	*summat*	*something*
art?	*are you?*	*tha's*	*you are, that is*
arta?	*are you?*	*tha's wha'*	*that is what*
does't?	*do you?*	*thee*	*you*
'er	*she, her*	*theer*	*there*
er's	*she is*	*thowt* ·	*thought*
gie	*give*	*thysen*	*yourself*
gorra	*got, must*	*toneet*	*tonight*
has't?	*do you have?*	*wha'sta?*	*what is it?*
'e 'issen	*he himself*	*wha's up?*	*what is the matter?*
leet	*light*	*weer's?*	*where is? where have?*
mun	*must' must not*		*where are?*
mysen	*myself*	*whacky*	*silly, mad*
nay	*no*	*wi'*	*with*
neet	*night*	*wi'out*	*without*
nowt	*nothing*	*wom*	*home*
nowty	*angry, bad-tempered*	*woulds't?*	*would you?*
o'er	*over*		

155